AND THEN NO
IN
Praise

It was only a matter of time before ~~~~ audience for whom *Exile on Main* ~~~~ and worthy of study as *The Catche* ~~~~ ...... The series ... is freewheeling and eclectic, ran~~~~ from minute rock-geek analysis to idiosyncratic personal celebration—*The New York Times Book Review*

Ideal for the rock geek who thinks liner notes just aren't enough—*Rolling Stone*

One of the coolest publishing imprints on the planet—*Bookslut*

These are for the insane collectors out there who appreciate fantastic design, well-executed thinking, and things that make your house look cool. Each volume in this series takes a seminal album and breaks it down in startling minutiae. We love these. We are huge nerds—*Vice*

A brilliant series ... each one a work of real love—*NME* (UK)

Passionate, obsessive, and smart—*Nylon*

Religious tracts for the rock "n" roll faithful—*Boldtype*

[A] consistently excellent series—*Uncut* (UK)

We ... aren't naive enough to think that we're your only source for reading about music (but if we had our way ... watch out). For those of you who really like to know everything there is to know about an album, you'd do well to check out Bloomsbury's "33 1/3" series of books—*Pitchfork*

For almost 20 years, the 33-and-a-Third series of music books has focused on individual albums by acts well known (Bob Dylan, Nirvana, Abba, Radiohead), cultish (Neutral Milk Hotel, Throbbing Gristle, Wire), and many levels in-between. The range of music and their creators defines "eclectic," while the writing veers from freewheeling to acutely insightful. In essence, the books are for the music fan who (as Rolling Stone noted) "thinks liner notes just aren't enough."—*The Irish Times*

For reviews of individual titles in the series, please visit our blog at 333sound.com
and our website at http://www.bloomsbury.com/musicandsoundstudies

Follow us on Twitter: @333books

Like us on Facebook: https://www.facebook.com/33.3books

For a complete list of books in this series, see the back of this book.

Forthcoming in the series:

Shout at the Devil by Micco Caporale
I'm Wide Awake, It's Morning by Holden Seidlitz
Re by Carmelo Esterrich
New Amerykah Part Two (Return of the Ankh)
by Kameryn Alexa Carter
Tragic Kingdom by Rhae Lynn Barnes
The Land of Rape and Honey by Jason Pettigrew
Blue Bell Knoll by Chris Tapley
and many more …

And Then Nothing Turned Itself Inside-Out

Elliott Simpson

BLOOMSBURY ACADEMIC
NEW YORK • LONDON • OXFORD • NEW DELHI • SYDNEY

BLOOMSBURY ACADEMIC
Bloomsbury Publishing Inc
1385 Broadway, New York, NY 10018, USA
50 Bedford Square, London, WC1B 3DP, UK
29 Earlsfort Terrace, Dublin 2, Ireland

BLOOMSBURY, BLOOMSBURY ACADEMIC and the Diana logo are
trademarks of Bloomsbury Publishing Plc

First published in the United States of America 2025

Library of Congress Cataloging-in-Publication Data
Names: Simpson, Elliott, author.
Title: And then nothing turned itself inside-out / Elliott Simpson.
Other titles: Yo La Tengo's And then nothing turned itself inside-out
Description: [1.] | New York : Bloomsbury Academic, 2025. |
Series: 33 1/3 | Includes bibliographical references.
Identifiers: LCCN 2024029365 (print) | LCCN 2024029366 (ebook) |
ISBN 9798765106679 (paperback) | ISBN 9798765106686 (ebook) |
ISBN 9798765106693 (pdf)
Subjects: LCSH: Yo La Tengo (Musical group). And then nothing turned itself
inside-out. | Indie pop music–United States–History and criticism. |
Rock music–United States–1991-2000–History and criticism.
Classification: LCC ML421.Y6 S56 2025 (print) | LCC ML421.Y6 (ebook) |
DDC 782.42164092/2–dc23/eng/20240725
LC record available at https://lccn.loc.gov/2024029365
LC ebook record available at https://lccn.loc.gov/2024029366

ISBN: PB: 979-8-7651-0667-9
          ePDF: 979-8-7651-0669-3
          eBook: 979-8-7651-0668-6

Series: 33 1/3

Typeset by Integra Software Services Pvt. Ltd.
Printed and bound in Great Britain

To find out more about our authors and books visit www.bloomsbury.com
and sign up for our newsletters.

Contents

Introduction   1

Everyday   9
Our Way to Fall   27
Let's Save Tony Orlando's House   43
Last Days of Disco   59
Nothing Turned Itself Inside Out ...   75
... And Became Something   87
Night Falls on Hoboken   97

Acknowledgments   107
Notes   108

Introduction

Bands aren't meant to be happy, and bands aren't meant to last.

Both of these things seemed like undeniable truths when I was growing up. The two groups my mum played around the house most often were The Beatles and Oasis, which had a huge impact on my perception of not only how bands were supposed to sound, but also how they were supposed to behave. For both of these acts, their stories and behind-the-scenes drama seemed just as important as their actual music, if not more so. When you hear the name Oasis, you're just as likely to envision the Gallagher brothers hurling insults at each other in the press as you are to think of "Wonderwall." And despite there being so many Beatles songs that have virtually become standards, everything that surrounds their music feels just as essential: the story of the band playing in Hamburg clubs for months on end, the rivalry between Paul McCartney and John Lennon, their final rooftop performance—this type of mythology felt critical to me. How could I care about a band, or their music, if there wasn't some drama-laden backstory propping it all up?

With this in mind, it really doesn't make sense for me to love Yo La Tengo as much as I do. Once described by *Rolling Stone* as doing for marriage what the Velvet Underground did for heroin,[1] Yo La Tengo is the antithesis of the romanticized self-destructing band. Formed by future husband and wife Ira Kaplan and Georgia Hubley in 1984, the group has gone on to become a symbol of consistency and stability in the indie rock world. Throughout their forty years, Yo La Tengo has never gone on hiatus, never let more than a couple years go by without releasing a new album or EP, and never let a single year pass without playing a show. Even in 2020, a particularly tricky year for touring, the band managed to pull off two socially distanced performances at the Massachusetts Museum of Contemporary Art. They have also been signed to the same record label and maintained the same lineup for the last thirty-or-so years, with bassist James McNew rounding out the trio.

Compared with acts like The Beatles and Oasis, there's something subversive about this stability. It's as if Yo La Tengo isn't, in fact, a band but instead a family-run business, a comparison that only makes more sense the deeper you dig. In a 2000 interview, Ira quipped that he and Georgia pretty much treat Yo La Tengo as their day jobs,[2] with their duties extending far beyond simply writing and recording music, and playing it live. Since the mid-nineties the band has been completely self-managed, which has required its three members to dabble in a range of disciplines. It has forced them to learn how to read contracts, become amateur accountants, and get to grips with the various ins and outs of music licensing. Up until the pandemic, they even worked the merch table at most of their shows, which, it is worth pointing out, normally features T-shirts designed by James. All this goes a long way toward painting the members of Yo La Tengo as ordinary, working people… Almost *anti*-rockstars. You're unlikely to spot Ira, Georgia, or James trashing a hotel room or throwing insults at each other in the press. Instead, you'll find them at home watching *Simpsons* reruns or browsing through second-hand shops for obscure seven-inches. And there's something incredibly endearing about that.

Of course, none of this would really matter if the music Yo La Tengo released wasn't uniformly great. Over the course of their career, the band has put out seventeen albums, a dozen-or-so EPs, several collaborative releases and film scores, a handful of B-side and rarity compilations, and a single album under their scuzzy alter-ego Condo Fucks. Not only have the majority of these releases been great, but unlike other bands that have been around for a similar length of time, there's never been a significant drop-off in quality. Yo La Tengo's most recent album, 2023's *This Stupid World*, stands toe-to-toe with their older work; from the gossamer-delicate ballad "Aselestine" to the doomy drone of the title track, it shows the group is far from running out of new ways to contort their sound. "It's a remarkable feat for a band this far down the road to create something that feels like a potential classic," Michael James Hall wrote in his *Under the Radar* review of the album,[3] while Jem Aswad, in his review for *Variety*, described it as a "new peak" for the band.[4] Somehow, despite being around for four decades, Yo La Tengo has managed to avoid transitioning into a legacy act. Each new release feels just as indispensable as the last one.

Another key aspect of the group's continued success is their reputation as an essential live act. While most bands mellow with age, their setlists slowly morphing into a predictable, unchanging greatest hits roll call, Yo La Tengo have only become wilder in their later years. Part of the thrill of seeing them live is that you never know what you're going to get; they might deliver an on-the-fly cover of an old Beach Boys song or pull out an obscure B-side from the eighties they haven't played in twenty years— it's impossible to predict. On their 2023 tour behind *This Stupid World*, the band played over 200 different songs across sixty-six shows, including 140 different covers.[5] This makes every performance a rewarding experience for dedicated fans; no matter which song you're hoping for—even if it's the Looney Tunes theme—there's always a chance that they'll bust it out. In a way, this encapsulates how Yo La Tengo have managed to stay such a vital band for so long: they always stay true to themselves. Every time they record a new album or play a show, they listen to themselves first and their audience second, always following their own instincts. As Ira puts it, "We try to be a band that we would like."[6]

Few acts have survived for as long as Yo La Tengo, even fewer have remained as consistently interesting as them over that time, and that, in itself, feels like its own incredible story. In this book, through the lens of one album, I'll explore just how Yo La Tengo have managed to construct such an enviable, long-lasting career and how their approach suggests good music doesn't come from drama and conflict, but quiet, steady work.

When telling the band's unique story, their 2000 album *And Then Nothing Turned Itself Inside-Out* is essential. The album was released at an important juncture in their career. After sixteen years of making music, Yo La Tengo had slowly swollen into a big name in the indie rock sphere. Their previous album, *I Can Hear the Heart Beating as One*, saw them reach a larger audience than ever before—becoming their first release to land on Billboard's Heatseekers Albums chart—and contains several of their most enduring songs, including "Autumn Sweater" and "Sugarcube." While this burst of success wasn't seismic in the context of the wider music world, it definitely shook up the band's visibility, as James McNew notes: "We were rolling all the time, and going back and forth to festivals in Europe and stuff that we hadn't been asked to play before—or actually, had been asked *not* to play previously."[7] They were declared by *Pitchfork*, then only a few years old, to be "the greatest band in the universe."[8]

That album's follow-up could have acted as a launchpad for Yo La Tengo to grow even bigger—to make a run at true commercial success—but instead *And Then Nothing* saw them retreat into themselves. The 77-minute album is filled with hushed, wintery songs that rarely rise above a whisper. Thematically, the album is similarly subdued; Ira and Georgia's lyrics explore the ennui and beauty that can emerge from everyday life, with topics ranging from uneventful weekends spent watching TV ("Saturday") to late-night spousal arguments ("From Black to Blue"). For a band that was also becoming known for their unpredictable live shows, led by Ira's wild guitar antics, the decision to put out something so contemplative, so slow to reveal itself, definitely seemed like a risk. It was a display of Yo La Tengo's commitment to doing what felt right to them rather than what their growing audience expected. And it's decisions like these—Yo La Tengo prioritizing being a band that they would like—that have ultimately come to define their career. More than any of their other releases, *And Then Nothing Turned Itself Inside-Out* established them as artists who want to achieve success on their own terms.

I would argue that the context surrounding the album's release is just as important as the music itself. Appearing in the year 2000, *And Then Nothing* not only arrived during a significant point of transition for the band, but also the music industry as a whole. Released the previous year, Napster was beginning to reshape things dramatically, causing the power of the album as a physical product to wane in a way that it would never recover from. Yo La Tengo is a band that benefitted from the music industry boom of the nineties and their continued success was not guaranteed in the new millennium. Rather than fighting against the changing times, as many other artists chose to do, the band instead doubled down on what they had been doing up until that point: listening to themselves. In this way, their philosophy and approach to being a band mirror the themes of *And Then Nothing* perfectly: the need to push forward through the struggles of the everyday and strive for those rare moments of beauty, even when they don't come easily. This is what makes it the perfect lens through which to view the band's larger story.

The structure of the book will reflect this, progressing through the album's themes and songs while simultaneously chronicling Yo La Tengo's journey as a band. We'll start with *And Then Nothing*'s opener, "Everyday," which explores a fear of routine and stagnation—something the group have always fought against—through droning instrumentation and serenely detached vocals. Love, in a muted and ordinary form, is another key theme of the album and Yo La Tengo's career as a whole. We see this through songs like "Our Way to Fall" and "The Crying of Lot G," which, if they don't directly depict Kaplan and Hubley's relationship, echo the ways it has served as the band's indestructible core for the entirety of its existence. On other tracks like "You Can Have It All"—a souped-up cover of a seventies disco deep cut—Yo La Tengo demonstrate their unmatched ability to mine the history of popular music and use it to shape their own identity. *And Then Nothing Turned Itself Inside-Out* is an important release not only because it feels like a culmination of the band's journey up until that point, but also because it set them up for the second half of their career. The success of the album—a left-turn for the band at such a crucial point in their career—confirmed to Ira, Georgia, and James that the only people they really needed validation from was themselves.

Yo La Tengo's refusal to compromise their creative and professional values over a forty-year career demands the attention of anyone interested in the history of indie rock. This book will not only function as an examination of one of the most astonishing albums of the 2000s and the band that created it, but also as an exploration of what great art is and the environment needed to produce it. As we'll find out, even when it seems like you have nothing at first, nothing can turn itself inside-out and become something.

Everyday

Routine has never sounded more ominous than on "Everyday," the first track on *And Then Nothing Turned Itself Inside-Out*. Opening with an incessant buzz that resembles the hum of a fluorescent light, the song builds slowly and darkly. Next come the hollow-sounding drums and a looping bassline that continually ascends and descends. The music has an anxious energy to it; it's the sound of lying awake at two o'clock in the morning, your mind whirring while everything else in the world remains still and quiet. When all the instruments are present and the mood is set, Georgia's voice finally emerges.

"I wanna cross my heart, I wanna hope to die," she sings, almost monotone, her vocals mirroring the energy of the music it sits above. In fact, if her voice is above the music, it's only by a couple of inches, as for most of the song it sounds like she's wading through it, just managing to keep her head above water. The song's musical stagnancy, continually circling the same notes, reflects the monotony of everyday life that Georgia explores in the lyrics. She wants everything and nothing to change, craving a more exciting life but also hoping that Tuesday is exactly the same as Monday. Eventually, the song sinks into a single refrain, "Looking to embrace the nothing of everyday," and then, finally, every word falls away except that last one. *Everyday, everyday, everyday*, chanted over and over until the song finally peters out.

It's a bold move to open your album with its dreariest moment. But at the same time, it makes perfect sense. "Everyday," depending on how you react to it, either serves as an invitation into the world of *And Then Nothing* or a final warning to get off the ride before it properly begins. The uneasiness given off by the song is central to the album in many ways. Though it's not at the forefront of every song, you can always at least sense it humming along in the background. It makes the moments of small, tender beauty all the more stunning. In the context of a louder album, songs like "Our Way to Fall" and "You Can Have It All" would get crushed between the big singles. In the world of *And Then Nothing*, they're allowed to shine. They're the sun breaking through the clouds, a representation of the bright moments many of us hope to stumble upon as we wade through the everyday.

Of course, even before the opening buzz of "Everyday" hits you, the album's central theme has already been clearly laid out. Its title, *And Then Nothing Turned Itself Inside-Out*, is drawn from a quote by legendary experimental jazz musician Sun Ra, who Yo La Tengo have covered many times over the years. Looking at Sun Ra's original quote, the album's title makes even more sense: "At first there was nothing then nothing turned itself inside-out and became something."[1] It showcases the album's central contrast, between nothing and something, and how the former can turn into the latter when you least expect it.

And then there's the album art, which, like any good cover, sums up the music behind it impeccably. It depicts a nondescript residential street in the dead of night. Off to the far right, a man stands alone, shopping bag in hand, gazing up at a dazzling lightbeam. Whether an alien abduction is about to take place, or a conversation with God, it's impossible to know. Taken from photographer Gregory Crewdson's *Twilight* series, the image known as "Untitled (beer dream)" captures both the claustrophobia of suburban living and the momentary flickers of wonder that can come out of it. This theme has acted as a thread through most of Crewdson's work; his cinematic photos are always lavishly arranged, often leveraging professional film sets, and attempt to transform ordinary, everyday environments into something larger than life. As he puts it in an interview with *The American Reader*, "It's not enough for it just to be strange or mysterious, it also has to feel very ordinary, very familiar, and very nondescript."[2] The cover for *And Then Nothing* is built around this contrast. Ordinary: uniform houses, pristine lawns, and parked cars. Extraordinary: a spotlight coming down from the sky. When comparing the album's cover with the original photo, you can see how much of this extraordinary section was cut off. Nearly cropped out of the composition entirely, it looks like something the photographer captured by accident, leaving more mysteries than even the famously enigmatic Crewdson would allow. Still, that slight glimpse of the man with the shopping bag, enveloped by a beam of light, is absolutely essential to the story the album is telling.

This ordinary/extraordinary contrast is a theme that pops up again and again on *And Then Nothing Turned Itself Inside-Out*. The album constantly flips between these two states, as shown by its opening songs. "Our Way to Fall," which follows the sonic dirge of "Everyday" is, by contrast, light and pretty. A love song with disarmingly straightforward lyrics about falling for someone, it feels weightless in the same way that "Everyday" feels heavy. The two songs seem to be in conversation with each other, enforced by the fact that they feature different lead vocalists. Whereas "Everyday" opens with Georgia remarking that she wants summer's sad songs behind her, "Our Way to Fall" starts with Ira warmly reminiscing about a summer's day. Both of them seem to be interacting with the same memory—they're just looking at it from different angles.

As if to further accentuate the song's delicate beauty, "Our Way to Fall" is followed by another of the album's most despondent songs: "Saturday." This time, Georgia and Ira sing it together. The song is colored by the steady chug of a Casio drum machine, which rattles along like a slow-moving train. The rest of the instruments on "Saturday" feel restless, constantly fidgeting, creating a claustrophobic mood that resembles the party Georgia describes in the first verse: "The room was filled with talk for anyone listening." If "Everyday" explores how monotonous weekdays can be, flitting by like scenery through a car window, then "Saturday" suggests that the weekend, despite all its promises, can just be more of the same. In the final verse of the song, we see Georgia absent-mindedly engaging in an activity synonymous with the suburban landscapes depicted in Crewdson's photography: watching TV. "I was engrossed in the film without really watching," she sings. "Said, 'Who's the guy with the gun?' as if I was involved."

***

Though Ira and Georgia were raised in vastly different worlds—Georgia in the heart of Manhattan and Ira in Croton-on-Hudson, a village in upstate New York—both of their upbringings reflect the themes and music of *And Then Nothing*. In particular, Ira's childhood seems likely to have informed the ordinary in the album's central ordinary/extraordinary contrast. Ira's family life has been described as exuding "a postwar suburban normal,"[3] hinting at a sixties American childhood that was filled with the familiar iconography seen in Crewdson's photography. And like a lot of kids who grew up around the same time, the extraordinary aspect of Ira's world was music, starting with The Beatles' first performance on *The Ed Sullivan Show*. It's a moment that galvanized dozens of other future famous musicians, including Billy Joel and Tom Petty, so it's hardly surprising that it inspired a young Ira Kaplan as well.

Things grew from there and soon the world of music Ira wanted to be a part of expanded beyond the confines of his parents' living room and into something more tangible, and certainly more extraordinary: New York City. Echoing the train-like drum machine that chugs through "Saturday," a teenage Ira learned that he could travel from North Croton Station to Grand Central on a $2.50 return ticket, allowing him to see many of the most essential underground acts of the seventies, including Television, Talking Heads, Patti

Smith, and the Ramones. It seemed clear to Ira that this was where he was meant to be, and it didn't take long for him to find a job that perfectly complemented his ever-growing obsession: music journalist.

Writing for publications such as the *SoHo Weekly* and *New York Rocker*, Ira's new career allowed him to be part of the music scene long before Yo La Tengo was a name anyone had heard of. Like an indie-rock Forrest Gump, Ira experienced countless "I was there" moments during his time as a music journalist; for example, both he and Georgia were at the filming of Bruce Springsteen's "Glory Days" music video. "Georgia's easy to spot," he says in a 2013 interview. "It's the end of the song, when all the E Street Band and Springsteen are throwing their fists in the air on two and four, and everybody in the audience is doing it as well. And just look for the one person that's not doing it and that's Georgia."[4]

In comparison to Ira, Georgia's childhood took place in the center of a creative world; it wasn't something she even had to switch on the TV to find. Her parents, John and Faith Hubley, were both celebrated animators, with their 1962 short film *The Hole* winning that year's Academy Award for Best Animated Short Film. As Georgia's sister, Emily, describes it, their parents were workaholics, but in a way in which they strived to spend as much time with their children as possible. "When we were young, they would bring us in to color things," Emily says. "We'd work at the studio over the summer as soon as we were old enough to use the markers."[5] Georgia and her siblings lent their voices to a number of their parents' short films as well. Essentially, the Hubleys' work and home lives were blended together as one.

This provided Georgia with an environment where she was able to flourish creatively. In a 1997 interview with *New York Magazine*, Georgia recalls how she was allowed to practice the drums in the Madison Avenue warehouse her parents used as their animation studio. Her playing attracted the attention of the manager of the Carlyle Hotel across the street, who, fearing Georgia's drumming would disturb his guests, tried to bribe Faith into stopping her daughter from practicing. "She's pursuing her art, and she has the right to do that," Faith responded, "and we don't need your money, thank you very much."[6]

These formative experiences seemed to have influenced not only the music Yo La Tengo makes but also how they operate as a band. It's easy to see how the way that John and Faith Hubley functioned as a creative couple, running their own animation studio together, informed Yo La Tengo's ethos, with Ira and Georgia's relationship acting as the band's stable core. Also taking into account James McNew, who has been the band's bassist since 1992, it's remarkable how impervious to change the group have stayed. This is because they understand the balance needed to maintain a creative career. Their relative ordinariness as people, combined with an intense work ethic, is what has allowed them to create such extraordinary art and succeed in having such a long and fruitful career.

***

When reviewing an album or interviewing a band, it's helpful to have an angle in mind. It could be anything—where the members are from, what they sing about, who their biggest influences are—but it makes the writing process a whole lot easier. The issue for bands that have a couple at their center is that the relationship angle will sometimes be the only one that critics choose to take, which can lead to the two things being conflated. This is something that Yo La Tengo has had to contend with and push back against for almost the entirety of their career: Yo La Tengo the band and Ira and Georgia the couple are not the same thing.

This happened frequently during the press cycle for *And Then Nothing*, with the album's stripped-back presentation placing more emphasis on the band's lyrics than ever before. "Ira Kaplan and Georgia Hubley celebrate their indie rock marriage with Yo La Tengo's most beautiful album,"[7] opened an article in the *Cleveland Scene*, while an *Entertainment Weekly* review compared the album to "eavesdropping on a whispered late-night conversation"[8] between the two band members. When asked about the lyrics on *And Then Nothing*, Yo La Tengo was always quick to shut down the purely autobiographical readings some journalists had. "Things that resonate for the listener are there," Ira notes in one interview. "It doesn't have to be what the lyrics mean to me. Our lyrics are not ripped from the pages of our diaries—but they are personal and they do represent our feelings."[9]

There has always been an inherently confessional quality to lyric-led music, whether it's a finger-picked folk song or a big pop number. We like to believe the singer is telling us, and only us, their deepest, darkest secrets, which can cause the line between autobiography and fiction to feel blurry. More than any of Yo La Tengo's previous albums, *And Then Nothing* invited listeners to scrutinize its lyrics simply because of its intimate construction. Apart from the shoegaze-inflected "Cherry Chapstick," the music here is uniformly restrained and quiet, so quiet that it often sounds as though Ira and Georgia are whispering directly into your ear. This imbues every line with importance; it almost doesn't matter how throwaway some of them were intended to be when originally written—the presentation makes them meaningful.

Listening to *And Then Nothing Turned Itself Inside-Out*, it's very easy to feel like you know Ira and Georgia, and the various ins and outs of their relationship, when that really isn't true at all. This explains why some journalists ended up crossing the line when interviewing the couple about the album, with the most telling example coming from a *New York Times* article by Kerry Lauerman. Toward the end of their conversation, Lauerman asks Ira and Georgia if they've thought about putting the band on hold and having children in the near future. Georgia's response is sharp: "That's none of your business. My mother doesn't even know the answer to that question."[10]

When examining the lyrics on *And Then Nothing*, it's important to bear in mind Ira's point: the lyrics are personal and they do represent the band members' feelings, yes, but they shouldn't be seen as diary entries. When you listen to "Our Way to Fall," the song's truth is the feeling of longing and warmth that swells in your stomach, not how it explicitly relates to Ira and Georgia's relationship. The same applies to "Saturday" and the vortex of dread it conjures up. It's also important to consider that there are songs that don't support the album's overall reputation as an intimate, confessional piece of art. "Let's Save Tony Orlando's House," for example, details a pyromaniacal conflict between sixties pop singers Tony Orlando and Frankie Vallie, while "Cherry Chapstick" sees Ira rhapsodizing about a girl next door who's wearing nothing except the titular lip balm. The worlds of these songs exist in an entirely separate universe from Ira and Georgia's relationship.

Still, the emotional truths explored in *And Then Nothing*, and its central balance between the ordinary and extraordinary, seem to reflect so much of Yo La Tengo's emotional journey as a band. Just as we see the characters on the album flicker between detached numbness ("Everyday") and vivid, emotional highs ("Our Way to Fall"), Yo La Tengo's route from utter unknowns to a band whose music warranted so much scrutiny from the press was one of them learning how to open up and be themselves.

As much as Ira and Georgia's marriage exists separately from Yo La Tengo, the origins of the band are very much tied up with the origins of their relationship. It all started with them. And it's likely that if they hadn't crossed paths, then not only would Yo La Tengo never have existed, but neither of them might have ever made it on stage as musicians. Both Ira and Georgia were incredibly timid people, and the support and encouragement they gave each other proved crucial. "We were drawn to each other because we could recognize the same certain shyness in each other," Georgia notes. "We both really wanted to get over that, but it was very hard at first. It still is, sometimes."[11]

As you might expect, it was a love of music that drew them together; the two of them met at a Feelies show at Danceteria, the famous Manhattan club. "We had mutual friends and mutual interests in bands that didn't have particularly large followings," Ira says. "So it was kind of inevitable that we would meet up at some point."[12] It wasn't long after becoming a couple that the two of them decided to try making music together. Georgia had been playing drums since she was a kid and Ira spent a lot of his spare time noodling on guitars, so it made sense for them to give it a shot.

The journey from their first practice session together to eventually forming Yo La Tengo was slow and hesitant. Perhaps the third most important element in the group's formation—after Ira and Georgia themselves—was the legendary Hoboken music venue, Maxwell's. Founded by Steve Fallon in 1979, Maxwell's quickly became an indispensable part of the Hoboken music scene; it was a place where many of the biggest indie rock acts of the eighties and nineties played some of their earliest shows, including Nirvana, R.E.M., the Replacements, and Minutemen. This was enough to make sure Ira and Georgia went there frequently. Though they started off as gig attendees, the two of them soon began working at the club, with Ira doing sound and Georgia occasionally DJing. Maxwell's quickly became an intrinsic part of their lives, so much so that they decided to move to Hoboken specifically because of the venue. Equally telling is the fact that the two of them only decided to move back to Manhattan after the club closed its doors for good in 2013.

The musical community that surrounded them in Maxwell's gave the young couple the confidence they needed as musicians. And when the opportunity finally arose for them to perform in front of an audience, they took it. The original iteration of Yo La Tengo—known as Georgia & Those Guys—played their first show in 1983 to celebrate the birthday of Maxwell's bartender Bill Ryan. This version of the band featured Ira, Georgia, and a revolving cast of guest performers, and only played covers; their setlists included everything from the Velvet Underground to Meat Puppets and KISS. As they slowly started taking themselves more seriously, Georgia & Those Guys morphed into A Worrying Thing and then, in 1984, Yo La Tengo. Finally, Ira and Georgia had a real band.

***

As with Georgia & Those Guys, Yo La Tengo's first performance took place at Maxwell's. In addition to Ira on rhythm guitar and Georgia on drums, the original lineup also featured Dave Schramm on lead guitar and Dave Rick on bass. The band's first single, "The River of Water"—released just a few months after their debut show—offers a glimpse of what they sounded like in those early days. Resembling the band that first brought Ira and Georgia together—the Feelies—they are almost completely unrecognizable as the musicians that would go on to record *And Then Nothing Turned Itself Inside-Out* a decade-and-a-half later.

While many great bands come out of the gate fully formed, like Ira and Georgia's heroes the Velvet Underground, "The River of Water" is evidence that this doesn't always happen. The song is by no means awful, but it lacks the distinct voice that Yo La Tengo would slowly cultivate over the ensuing years. Even though they are finally recording music together, it still sounds like Ira and Georgia are trying to hide themselves away. With lyrics that lack any real sense of personality, Ira sings in vague clichés while Dave Schramm's showy lead guitar, though impressive, feels like it's only there to smother the couple's own instruments and insecurities. Listening to "The River of Water," it's unclear what we're supposed to come away feeling. The emotional pull is missing.

When interviewing the band about *And Then Nothing*, Mark Athitakis used the word "intimate" to describe the album. As soon as the word was uttered, Ira latched onto it as a way to chart how Yo La Tengo's sound had evolved over time. "We're probably less consciously afraid of that," he says. "I think in years past there would have been a greater reluctance to open ourselves up as much as we are willing to open ourselves up now."[13] Intimate also feels like a key word when describing what's missing from "The River of Water" and much of the band's early material. In many ways, the sixteen-year journey from "The River of Water" to *And Then Nothing* is one of Ira and Georgia learning how to be more vulnerable in the music they produce.

This is something you can see not only in the lyrics, but also in the musical presentation of the songs on *And Then Nothing*. "Saturday," one of the album's busiest moments, is a great example of this. The track's core is simple—another chugging drum machine and sparse bassline—but the more you listen to it, the more you realize how much else is going on. As the song builds, different elements shift in and out of focus. There are shakers, tinkling chimes, the low hum of an organ, and, at one point, what sounds like a cat running across a set of piano keys. When listening to it on headphones, the song almost sounds claustrophobic at times, keenly reflecting Georgia's anxious lyrics. This busyness feels artful, a way of conveying a specific feeling. However, as mentioned, the busyness on "The River of Water" just feels like a way for the band to drown out their insecurities and lack of finesse. The lead guitar and horns are only there as a form of protection.

Yo La Tengo went on to release three albums during the eighties through Coyote Records. Slightly tellingly, it's been over twenty years since any of these albums have received a rerelease. It's possible that some fans don't even know the group's career stretches back this far; for many, their sixth album, 1996's *Painful*, is seen as the point when Yo La Tengo truly became Yo La Tengo. Still, even if these first three albums aren't considered essential listens, they feature flickers of greatness. I'd describe them as stepping stones: small, incremental leaps that helped Yo La Tengo grow into the band we know and love today.

Still, even on their jangly 1986 debut, *Ride the Tiger*, we can see glimpses of the band that would go on to produce *And Then Nothing* fourteen years later. Ira's distinctive croon, while not quite fully formed, is very much present, as is his love of reverb-drenched guitars. Then, with 1987's *New Wave Hot Dogs*, which saw them shift toward a more college-rock sound, additional Yo La Tengo characteristics began to emerge. With Dave Schramm leaving after *Ride the Tiger*, Yo La Tengo shrunk down to a tight guitar, bass, and drums three-piece—a mode in which they'd continue to operate for the rest of their career. Additionally, the album contains the first Yo La Tengo love song: "Did I Tell You." "I try not to wonder, or tell you that I'm not willing to wait," Ira sings on the song's chorus, "Cause deep in my heart I'm willing." It feels like a prototype for many of the band's future classics.

These small shifts and evolutions continued on the band's third and final album of the eighties, *President Yo La Tengo*, which saw Georgia sing for the first time. The backing vocals she provides on "Alyda" feel like a revelation, transforming a good song into a truly great one. Her voice has gone on to become such an essential part of Yo La Tengo's sound that it's hard to believe the band released two albums that didn't make use of it. Elsewhere on the record, "Drug Test" saw the band score their first college radio semi-hit. It's one of the most assured and catchy songs on the album, built around an ominous bassline and Ira's moody vocals. In an alternate universe where Yo La Tengo didn't survive past the eighties, this is the song they'd be remembered for.

As already outlined, one of the key contributors to Yo La Tengo's eventual success was their work ethic. Unlike many of their college-rock contemporaries—Hüsker Dü, Dinosaur Jr., the Replacements—Yo La Tengo didn't achieve any significant level of success in the eighties. Yet Ira and Georgia continued to play shows and release music at a regular clip, even as they held down other jobs. And it wasn't only success that eluded Yo La Tengo during its early days, but also a permanent bassist. By the time the nineties arrived, the group had already cycled through eleven different bass players, with their longest-lasting one, Stephen Wichnewski, sticking around for only three years. Many other bands would've given up at that point, but Yo La Tengo continued to soldier on, even if they still hadn't quite worked out what made them unique.

Many of the most interesting moments on these early albums come when the group take risks, like Georgia's backing vocals on "Alyda" or the ten-minute noise guitar freak-out of "The Evil That Men Do (Pablo's Version)." Over time, this risk-taking would turn into a key part of Yo La Tengo's approach as a band, giving them the confidence they needed to go with their gut. It's something that Ira sums up incredibly well in a 2020 interview: "I've always thought that a lot of the development of the band is confidence, and confidence to accept that, 'OK, this may not be anything like anything we've done before but that's alright.'"[14]

It's with their fourth album, *Fakebook*, that Yo La Tengo took their first significant risk as a band. Following the departure of another bassist, Georgia and Ira decided their next album should be more stripped back, consisting of eleven acoustic covers of some of their favorite songs (Daniel Johnston's "Speeding Motorcycle") and two reworkings of older Yo La Tengo songs ("Barnaby, Hardly Working," "Did I Tell You"), alongside a handful of new ones ("The Summer"). Following on from the college-rock distortion of *President Yo La Tengo*, it was a shift that didn't make much sense on paper. Why move so abruptly away from the sound people were just starting to recognize you for? And what kind of indie rock band does a cover album, let alone one with covers of their own songs? It was the first time that Yo La Tengo sharply pivoted away from what was happening in the indie rock scene and instead followed their instincts.

And the risk paid off. Not only did *Fakebook* generate more attention for the band than any of their previous albums—it saw them go on larger tours than ever before, even journeying out to Europe for the first time—but it felt like a huge success on an artistic level as well. Lead single "The Summer" was the first Yo La Tengo song to receive a music video, and it's not difficult to see why. Built around Ira and Georgia's harmonized voices and the chug of two acoustic guitars, it feels more assured than anything they'd put out up until that point. It's the sound of a band discovering themselves. Just like the songs on *And Then Nothing Turned Itself Inside-Out*, which so effortlessly beam Ira and Georgia's feelings into the listener's head, "The Summer" succeeds in capturing a specific mood—a warm sense of nostalgia. This is only accentuated by the accompanying music video, which splices together footage of Georgia and Ira whispering into each other's ears, watching ants crawl across fresh watermelons, and strumming guitars in daylight-flooded rooms. There's an ease to it that isn't present on their first three albums.

Part of *Fakebook*'s success can also be tied to the steady work that Ira and Georgia continued to put into the band. Though they weren't currently making enough for Yo La Tengo to serve as their full-time jobs, they treated it as such, making dozens of on-air radio appearances in promotion of the album. In this sense, we can see how *Fakebook*'s minimalist presentation was a clever business move as well as a creative one: Ira and Georgia didn't need a bassist to play these new songs, making it much easier for them to turn up to radio stations as a duo. Hard work and creativity, hand in hand. The ordinary and the extraordinary.

Our Way to Fall

Yo La Tengo's discography overflows with love songs and choosing a favorite is a near-impossible task. "Autumn Sweater" is a worthy contender. Built around two shuffling drum sets and a church-like organ, Ira tenderly croons about escaping a party to be alone with someone you have a crush on. Then there's "Nowhere Near," which effortlessly showcases the band's ability to transmit a mile-wide feeling through one simple line: "Everyone is here, but you're nowhere near." Or, if you prefer the band's later work, there's "I'll Be Around" from *Fade*. Prominently featured in the Richard Linklater film *Boyhood*, the song contains nothing more than a finger-picked guitar and Ira softly promising to stick around. If we widen the net to include the many, many covers of love songs that Yo La Tengo has recorded, then a dozen more incredible options reveal themselves. There's the band's gorgeous, stripped-down version of The Cure's "Friday I'm in Love," their delicate take on the Only Ones' "The Whole of the Law," and also their buoyant rendition of George McCrae's "You Can Have It All."

Still, if it was necessary to boil the band's discography down to a single love song—one representative moment—then "Our

Way to Fall" feels like the obvious choice. In many ways, it's the archetypal Yo La Tengo love song. Simple and discreet, it's colored primarily by the soft hiss of an organ, which sounds like it's on its last legs, and a tentative bassline. Then there's Georgia's reserved drum playing, which focuses almost entirely on the hi-hats. Everything has a gossamer-like delicacy to it, like the song might fall apart at any second. When Ira's voice finally emerges, after what feels like an eternity of waiting, he sings as if he's got a lump in his throat, as if he's making an admission of love that he fears might not be reciprocated. And it's only when the song's chorus comes in, when Georgia's voice rises up to meet his, that the listener can finally breathe out. "Cause we're on our way," they sing. "We're on our way to fall in love."

Those last two lines of the chorus pierce the listener like an arrow through the heart. Just like "Nowhere Near," they demonstrate Yo La Tengo's ability to capture an entire universe of emotion in a few choice words. The broad sentiment of those lines wouldn't work half as well if the verses before them didn't feel so specific; every line refers to a different memory, from the protagonist's shy face turning red to his love interest strumming The Who's "I Can't Explain" on an old guitar. It's that reference in particular that makes the characters in the song come to life. It reflects the intense relationship that all three Yo La Tengo members have with music, and how delicately their favorite songs are woven into their own life stories. "I Can't Explain," tellingly, was released in 1964—the same year that Ira was radicalized by The Beatles and the greater British Invasion.

Referencing other people's songs in their lyrics is something Yo La Tengo have always done and continue to do. "Big Day Coming" from *Painful* includes a mention of "Sittin' on a Fence" by the Rolling Stones, and "Brain Capers" from *This Stupid World* quotes both Ray Davies of the Kinks and Alice Cooper. It's a way for them to Trojan-horse sentiments from big rock numbers into their much quieter, contemplative songs. You could argue that "Our Way to Fall" addresses the same emotions as "I Can't Explain," only in a wildly different way. Hushed rather than explosive. Tip-tapping hi-hats instead of a thundering kick drum and a soft organ wheeze instead of a window-shattering guitar riff.

Given that Ira, Georgia, and James are all self-confessed music nerds, it only makes sense for them to use classic songs as shorthand for big emotions. And really, isn't that something we all do? The right song, when it hits you at the right time, can become so inextricably linked with what you were feeling at a particular moment. That's one of the most powerful things about music. It's the reason why so many couples have an "our song"—that one song that somehow manages to perfectly encapsulate their feelings for each other. For the characters in "Our Way to Fall," that song might be "I Can't Explain." And given how "Our Way to Fall" has ended up soundtracking the first dance at many people's weddings, it seems likely that it's become an "our song" for many couples as well.

***

And Then Nothing Turned Itself Inside-Out is an album filled with relationship songs. That's the main reason so many people clung to the narrative of it being about Ira and

Georgia's marriage. "Last Days of Disco" carries the same hesitant energy as "Our Way to Fall," with the protagonist detailing his first tentative foray into the world of dancing and the release he finds in moving with his partner. Then there's "You Can Have It All," the album's bossa-nova-inflected lead single, which sees Georgia sing as directly about love as she ever has. But *And Then Nothing*'s power as a relationship album comes from its ability to explore that theme from a number of perspectives. It understands that relationships don't run smoothly all the time, and so those tender moments are inevitably balanced out by small conflicts. It's what makes the characters that Ira and Georgia portray feel so real.

Following straight on from the budding romance of "Last Days of Disco," we get "The Crying of Lot G." The reference to Thomas Pynchon's 1966 novel *The Crying of Lot 49* in the title feels like a red herring more than anything else, with the song instead being a grounded examination of a couple's argument. Instrumentally, the song is typical of the album, assembled out of delayed guitar licks and a gentle, shuffling drumbeat. Both Ira and Georgia lend their voices to the song but take contrasting approaches. While Ira adopts a talk-singing mumble, Georgia's vocals are wordless and melodic, wrapping around Ira's lyrics like a soft blanket, gently easing the anxiety out of his voice.

"Expecting a whisper, I hear the slam of the door," Ira sings in the opening, immediately setting the scene. Over the course of the song, he attempts to dissect the argument he and his partner have found themselves in—trying to work out whose fault it is—before coming to the conclusion that, ultimately, it doesn't matter. He knows they'll make it through to the other side because their relationship is bigger than any one fight; it's as though he's marching through a storm without a coat or umbrella, comforted by the knowledge that there'll be blue skies on the other side.

Just like "Our Way to Fall" and "Nowhere Near," "The Crying of Lot G" reaches its climax with a couple of simple, beautifully resonant lines. Unlike those songs though, these lines don't arrive on the chorus but, instead, the outro, forcing the listener to make it all the way through to the end of the track before being granted any sense of resolution. "The way that I feel when you laugh is like laughing," Ira sings. "The way that I feel when you cry is so bad." Georgia's voice merges with Ira's for these final lines of the song, underlining them as a moment of reconciliation. They're arguing, yes, but they're also in the argument together.

This nuanced representation of love is one of *And Then Nothing*'s greatest strengths. Similar to the push and pull between ordinary and extraordinary seen in songs like "Everyday" and "Saturday," we can observe, here, shifts in the state of the fictional relationship that sits at the album's center. It almost feels like a collection of tender snapshots that have been collaged together to form a larger work. This is reinforced by the album's sequencing: the hesitant dance floor flirting of "Last Days of Disco" transitions easily into the argument of "The Crying of Lot G," which, after concluding with a moment of reconciliation, is followed by the unrestrained euphoria of "You Can Have It All." The tracklist feels like a textured landscape, complete with peaks and valleys.

Speaking to *MTV News* about *And Then Nothing*, Roger Moutenot—who produced all of the band's releases between

1993 and 2009—perfectly sums up the album's appeal. "It's simple, but it's from the heart," he says. "They're just very real people, and that's what comes across on the record. It's not like, 'Let's make a record to sell millions of copies.' It's like, 'This is who we are.'"[1] There's a lack of bombast to many of the songs on *And Then Nothing*, making the album's examination of love feel comfortingly ordinary. While a huge pop song is no less honest in its exploration of this theme, Yo La Tengo's investment in small, concrete details has always caused their music to resonate in a startlingly unique way.

Another song on the album that explores this bruised side of love is "From Black to Blue." Emerging from the fuzz of the previous track, the riff-heavy "Cherry Chapstick," it almost feels like a hangover after a heavy night. The song gradually shakes itself into shape, transforming into a warbling sea of reverb and distortion decorated with staccato keyboard stabs and woozy organ tones. "As the empty feeling turns from black to blue, I can't believe this never happens to you," Ira sings on the chorus. Like the couple in "The Crying of Lot G," it feels like an argument has just taken place and the protagonist is trying to recover their footing in the relationship. Though "From Black to Blue" doesn't conclude with the same sense of lyrical resolve as "The Crying of Lot G," the way James and Georgia's voices come in to join Ira's on the final chorus feels like its own resolution. It's as though the weight of Ira's emotions is lessened by the three of them agreeing to share it.

The way the song concludes also feels symbolic of Yo La Tengo's journey as a band. Even through the most difficult of times, the group's core trio always remains intact.

***

Though James doesn't provide any lead vocals on *And Then Nothing*, he played just as vital a role in the album's development as Ira and Georgia. You can feel his presence in every song, both through the many instruments he plays and the backing vocals he provides. His contribution to the album is something Ira went out of his way to stress in interviews around *And Then Nothing*'s release. "Because of the marriage, it's easy to overlook his contributions," Ira laments. "It's not our favourite part of reading things that are written about us. It's just inaccurate."[2]

At the time of *And Then Nothing*'s release, James had been a member of Yo La Tengo for almost nine years. And as I write this in 2024, he's been with the band for thirty-three of its forty years. So, as tempting as it is to home in on the couple narrative, all three members of Yo La Tengo are as indispensable as each other at this point. The fact that Ira and Georgia managed to shuffle through fourteen different bassists in the band's first eight years only makes James's long tenure more impressive. It's also telling that for all the band's releases since 1995, every song has been credited simply to "Yo La Tengo." As the title of their eighth album, *I Can Hear the Heart Beating as One,* suggests, the trio always move in unison with each other, as if they're simply the different limbs of a single organism.

James McNew didn't grow up in any one place. With his dad working as a traveling insurance salesman, his family moved around a lot during his childhood, something that probably helped prepare him for a life spent touring in a band. Like Ira and Georgia, James's obsession with music came early in his life. At around eight or nine, he started taking guitar lessons and from then on all he wanted to do was play in bands. After spending most of his teen years in Charlottesville working tedious service jobs, his first big break as a musician came when he was invited to join the indie rock band Christmas in 1989. "It was like Batman seeing the bat signal in the sky," James says. "It was crazy because they were my favourite band and they called me at my job and asked me to help them write some songs. It was like *wow*, dreams come true!"[3]

Not many people talk about Christmas these days. Though the group had many things in common with Yo La Tengo—Christmas's consistent core was guitarist Michael Cudahy and drummer Liz Cox—sound-wise they couldn't be more different. Christmas's music was much pricklier. Listening to the band's final album, *Vortex*, the only one to feature James, it can be difficult to find a steady foothold; many of the songs are built around odd time signatures and few feature a discernible hook. As James said though, playing with Michael and Liz was effectively a dream job for him. So after getting the call, he packed up his stuff, quit his job as a parking lot attendant, and moved to Las Vegas to join the band as their new bassist.

Unfortunately, it didn't take long for issues to start bubbling up. The other members of Christmas weren't interested in performing live—something James was very keen to do—and after the band finally finished their new album, their label I.R.S. rejected it. (*Vortex* would ultimately be released by Matador Records a few years later.) Still, it was through playing with Christmas that James first crossed paths with his future bandmates. Yo La

Tengo and Christmas performed together a few times in the late eighties and early nineties, and James very quickly became friends with Ira and Georgia, and a fan of their band. During one post-show conversation with the duo, James half-jokingly told them to give him a call if they ever needed a new bassist. It only took Ira and Georgia two weeks to take him up on that offer.

The original plan was for James to fill in temporarily, but he quickly found playing with Ira and Georgia to be a revelation. In comparison to the more demanding, technical bass playing Christmas's music required, Yo La Tengo was much looser. "It was a really different way of playing with a band," he says. "There were stretches of songs where we'd just go and keep going until we decided to move onto the next part, and we didn't know how long that was gonna be. That became a very exciting and important part of music for me."[4] It also became clear that James was the bassist Ira and Georgia had spent the last eight years searching for. A steady, mellow presence, both in terms of his playing style and personality, he balanced out the more energetic Ira. As Christmas started to fall apart, soon evolving into the neo-lounge act Combustible Edison, James decided to devote himself to Yo La Tengo full-time.

Though James played on and toured Yo La Tengo's next album, 1992's *May I Sing with Me*, in the words of Ira, he remained more of a hired gun at that stage. Still, the album saw the band continue to grow. There are plenty of fantastic moments on *May I Sing with Me*—"Upside Down" is far and away the catchiest single Yo La Tengo had released up to that point and "Mushroom Cloud of Hiss" remains one of their most unhinged rockers—but "Sleeping Pill" stands out as the album's most significant milestone. The first song that Ira, Georgia, and James wrote together as a trio, the nine-minute odyssey maps out the instrumental dynamic that Yo La Tengo would go on to utilize for many of their best songs: James's bassline hypnotically repetitious, Georgia's drumbeat steady, and Ira's guitar riffs wandering and ravenous.

In James, Ira and Georgia finally found someone who could match their ambition and work ethic. "We just started practicing and playing all the time," Ira says. "And even if we didn't have a show, we got together and practiced."[5] Essentially, as James became an official member of Yo La Tengo, the three of them began to treat the band as their day jobs. And through this, their confidence increased by leaps and bounds.

Those leaps and bounds are visible in the band's sixth album, 1993's *Painful*. For most people, this is the point where Yo La Tengo truly found their sound; there's arguably no bigger jump in quality in the band's discography than between *May I Sing with Me* and *Painful*. And the importance of this album is something that Yo La Tengo themselves recognize. For the band's thirtieth anniversary in 2013, *Painful* was the album they chose to reissue in celebration—not *Ride the Tiger,* not *President Yo La Tengo*, not *Fakebook*. "I think the band we are today is traceable to that record, more than any one that came before it," Ira says. "Those records before are something else."[6] In a sense, *Painful* can be considered Yo La Tengo's true debut album. A debut that arrived nine years, six albums, and fifteen bassists deep into their career.

Not only was *Painful* the band's first album to be written and recorded primarily as a trio, it was also their first one to be released on Matador Records, which has remained their home ever since. Founded by Chris Lombardi just four years earlier, Matador was still a fledgling indie label in 1993, but it was already beginning to make a name for itself. In 1992, the label put out Pavement's debut album *Slanted and Enchanted*, which—bolstered by a co-sign from the legendary BBC DJ John Peel—became an unexpected success, shifting around 80,000 units in its first year and even charting in the UK. Not bad for an independent label. The year after, Matador released Liz Phair's *Exile in Guyville*. With the album topping both *The Village Voice* and *Spin*'s end-of-the-year lists, it further solidified Matador's reputation as a label to watch.

There's no doubt that the timing of Yo La Tengo's jump to Matador benefitted *Painful* greatly. Even though the album didn't make quite as big of a splash as *Slanted and Enchanted* or *Exile in Guyville*, Yo La Tengo's new label provided them with a level of reach and credibility that their previous ones couldn't. It's also worth noting that Matador started partnering with Atlantic Records in 1993. Though this collaboration with a major label would ultimately be short-lived, it granted Matador a huge cash injection and access to an international distribution network, allowing them to give some of their releases over the next few years an extra push—*Painful* included. This is reflected by the album's lead single, "From a Motel 6," receiving not one but two music videos; the second was reportedly made after Atlantic Records executives complained that the first, directed by legendary indie filmmaker Hal Hartley, was too artsy to be shown on MTV. The band also ended up performing the single on *Late Night with Conan O'Brien*, marking their first late-night TV appearance. Despite how deep Yo La Tengo were into their career at this point, they were essentially being treated as a hot new act.

Another important first for the band with *Painful* was the involvement of producer Roger Moutenot. Up until that point, the band's albums had almost exclusively been produced by Gene Holder of Hoboken-based band the dBs. A friend of Ira and Georgia's, Holder had also served as Yo La Tengo's fill-in bassist from time to time. While having a friend produce your albums sounds like a good idea on paper, by the time it came to record *Painful*, Ira and Georgia realized that an outside voice might benefit them more. This is why Roger's involvement was such a game changer: Yo La Tengo didn't really know him personally, only that he'd collaborated with some big names. "Roger's résumé was awesome," Ira explains. "He had worked with Lou Reed *and* the Village People."[7]

While Yo La Tengo had been born out of the somewhat insular Hoboken music scene, only by moving beyond it were Ira and Georgia able to transform their band into something truly special. Between the increased involvement of James, the support of Matador Records, and the guidance and production of Roger Moutenot, Yo La Tengo had finally been pushed into the next stage of their career.

Painful is packed full of incredible songs. It's Yo La Tengo's first front-to-back classic and feels like a culmination of everything they'd done up to that point. The record's heavier tracks—like the fuzzed-out rocker "Double Dare"—feel like a refinement of what the band had been doing on *President Yo La Tengo*, while its softer moments—such as the hushed murmurings of "The Whole of the Law"—build on the foundations laid down by *Fakebook*. Then there's the album's closer, "I Heard You Looking," which sees the band jam on a single chord progression for several minutes, similar to *May I Sing with Me*'s "Sleeping Pill." Comparing these two songs, you can chart how much tighter and confident the band had grown in the space of just a couple of years.

This album also saw the band expand in new sonic directions. In particular, the introduction of an Ace Tone organ to their musical palette felt revelatory, with the instrument having a huge presence on the album's loudest tracks ("Sudden Organ") as well as its quietest ones ("Nowhere Near"). The Ace Tone's role in Yo La Tengo's sound is something that would only continue to grow with subsequent albums, as even a cursory listen to *And Then Nothing* will reveal.

Though there isn't a single bad track on *Painful*, there is one that's especially important: "Big Day Coming." Ira and Georgia knew it was something special as soon as they wrote it back in 1991—so much so that they apparently pushed themselves onto the bill of a show at Maxwell's just so they could try it out live. Though we can't know for sure what that original version of the song sounded like, it apparently took up the whole of their twenty-eight-minute set. The fact that they held the song back, keeping it off *May I Sing with Me*, just demonstrates the confidence Ira and Georgia had in its potential. They wanted to wait until they could get it just right.

And, really, confidence is the perfect word to use when describing "Big Day Coming." As mentioned in the previous chapter, Yo La Tengo's journey from *Ride the Tiger* to *And Then Nothing* is one of them learning to have confidence in themselves, to take risks, and be vulnerable in their music, and in that regard "Big Day Coming" felt like their biggest leap forward yet. The song's lyrics are tender and straightforward, focusing on small, concrete details that feel incredibly real. "I woke up early, couldn't go back to sleep," Ira sings, "'cause I'd been thinking of where it all would lead." There's something self-referential about those words, as if Ira is singing about Yo La Tengo itself. Though the band had achieved some minor success by 1991, Ira and Georgia couldn't be sure what the future held. The big day coming referenced in the song's title and chorus almost feels prophetic; it's like the duo were trying to manifest their own success, willing *Painful* to be the breakthrough that they'd been waiting for.

Like "Our Way to Fall," "Big Day Coming" is undeniably a love song. It's there in the subtle musical references; when Ira sings that he wants to hold Georgia's hand, he's nodding to one of the songs that The Beatles performed on *The Ed Sullivan Show* back in 1964. That said, "Big Day Coming" isn't just a love song about Ira and Georgia's relationship, but also an ode to Yo La Tengo itself and all that the band had come to represent. Again, the fact that they saved the song for *Painful*, their first album as a "real" band with a stable lineup, only seems to support this.

Further underlining the significance of "Big Day Coming," two versions of the song appear on *Painful*. The first, which opens the album, is built around a hazy organ drone. The song calls to mind the image of a still, waveless sea—it often feels like it isn't moving at all—with the looping bassline and sparse guitar adding to the pacific mood. You can imagine this version of "Big Day Coming" going on for twenty-eight minutes. The second version feels like the Mr. Hyde to the first one's Dr. Jekyll; arriving at the end of the album, it sees Ira turn the guitar distortion up to eleven and, instead of crooning the lyrics, he shouts them out menacingly. For any other band, having two versions of the same song on one album might seem like an unusual move, but for Yo La Tengo it epitomized their creative philosophy. While the band has experimented with a number of sounds during their four-decade career, if you were to boil it down to two, you could use these two versions of "Big Day Coming" as a guideline: soft and tender crooning versus heavy, blistering distortion.

For the last decade, this is how the band has organized their shows as well. Often forgoing a support act, Yo La Tengo instead plays two sets: one quiet and one loud. "Big Day Coming" is one of the few songs that can show up in either of them. This duality is one of the things that has come to define the band. And though they've recorded hundreds of songs since "Big Day Coming," you can generally place each of them either into the loud camp or the quiet one. In this way, the song feels not only like the start of the band's journey into more confident, vulnerable lyricism, but also the beginning of them consolidating and refining a sonic identity.

As previously mentioned, *Painful* wasn't a huge runaway success at the time—at least not on the same level as Matador's bestsellers from this period—but in retrospect its significance is undeniable. In a review of the album's 2013 reissue, *Pitchfork*'s Stuart Berman referred to *Painful* as the moment that Yo La Tengo's music turned "three dimensional,"[8] while *Stereogum*'s Michael Nelson described it as "a landmark release that sets the table for a great band's most impressive achievements."[9] Even in the eyes of the band, it almost seemed to invalidate everything else they'd recorded up to that point. "Anyone that said they liked our other records more than *Painful*," Ira says, "I'd just tell them that they're wrong."[10] It's funny to think that Yo La Tengo started drawing more attention from the outside world when their sound turned more inward. By focusing on making music for themselves and listening to their own feelings, they made a bigger splash than ever before.

And Then Nothing Turned Itself Inside-Out is an album full of relationship songs, yes, but that doesn't mean James isn't present in them. In fact, you could argue that the album's core emotional narrative—two people navigating a romantic relationship—also embodies the creative relationship shared by the three bandmates, in the same way that "Big Day Coming" seems to represent both Ira and Georgia's relationship and the band they founded together. Talking about Ira and Georgia in a 2020 interview, James says, "I understand how much they love music, and they understand how much I love music. That is the first and strongest thing that brought us together—immediately."[11] The three of them share a connection and that connection is what's propelled Yo La Tengo this far. In this sense, "Our Way to Fall" is as much about the trio's shared love for each other as it is about Ira and Georgia as a couple. Balanced with *And Then Nothing*'s more downbeat moments, such as "The Crying of Lot G" and "From Black to Blue," the album can be read as a reflection of the inevitable ups and downs of any creative partnership.

Let's Save Tony Orlando's House

And Then Nothing Turned Itself Inside-Out is an album concerned with the contrasts and contradictions that make up our everyday lives. We've explored this both through the album's fluctuation between ordinary and extraordinary moments, and its representation of relationships, which can similarly shift between extremes in an instant. To further understand this world of contrasts, it's necessary to dig deeper into one of the album's recurring motifs, a quintessential contradiction that appears right there on its cover: the suburbs.

Artists across all mediums have been obsessed with the suburbs for a long time—particularly those who grew up in them. This is because there's always been an inherent tension to the suburbs as a concept. On one hand, they conjure up a vision of a welcoming, neighborly community—backyard barbecues and kids playing in the streets—and on the other, they represent a very modern type of isolation—rows of bland, identical houses, and people trapped in their homes with nothing to do and nowhere to escape. "My childhood was picket fences, blue skies, red flowers, and cherry trees," David Lynch once said in an interview, "but then I would see millions of little ants swarming on the cherry tree, which had pitch oozing out of it."[1] It's an image that perfectly distils the key contrast between light and darkness. It's as though all you need to do is pick off the top layer of clean white paint to uncover the decay and rot underneath.

This fascination with the darker, more isolated version of suburbia was something that grew as the twentieth century moved along. Despite the huge amount of the media that conjured up an idyllic view of the suburbs—TV advertisements, American family sitcoms like *The Brady Bunch* and *Home Improvement*—there were dozens of artists who tried their best to scratch away at the paint. Sofia Coppola's *The Virgin Suicides*, which debuted the year before *And Then Nothing* was released, is one of the most famous examples of this. Illustrating the suburbs' dual personalities, Coppola colors her picturesque streets with a warm, rosy tint—reflecting the nostalgic gaze of the boys-turned-men who narrate the story—contrasting this with the eerie suicide pact that the film takes its title from. That same year, director Sam Mendes gave a similarly cynical and searching critique of suburban banality with the Best Picture-winning *American Beauty*, in which a middle-aged father undergoes a mid-life crisis and becomes infatuated with his daughter's best friend, rippling changes through his family.

Another important artist who mined this territory in the nineties is, of course, photographer Gregory Crewdson. There's something lavishly artificial about his work. Rather than taking photos on the street by himself, camera in hand, Crewdson's photo shoots involve huge Hollywood-esque setups, with a single picture often requiring an entire film crew and extensive lighting equipment. Similar to *The Virgin Suicides*, this hyper-real quality makes the worlds he creates feel familiar and supernaturally heightened at the same time.

Inspired by such film directors as David Lynch and Steven Spielberg, as well as the writer John Cheever, much of Crewdson's photography has focused on the suburbs as a symbol. This can be seen most clearly in *Twilight*, the exhibition from which Yo La Tengo extracted the cover art for *And Then Nothing Turned Itself Inside-Out*. Many of the photos in the *Twilight* series feature isolated individuals, and rarely does more than one actor appear at a time. Crewdson strands these characters in vast, empty spaces—like a flooded family home or a seemingly endless suburban street—and, in doing so, captures the false sense of togetherness that the suburbs have come to represent. The characters never seem fully aware of what's going on or where they are. Often, they just stand there, looking bewildered. The Crewdson photograph that decorates the inside of *And Then Nothing*'s gatefold is a good example of this. In it, we see a man lawn-mowing crop circles in the middle of the night. You get the impression that he doesn't even know why he's doing it.

As with any album art, *And Then Nothing*'s visuals color and haunt the music inside. The protagonists of songs like "Everyday" and "Saturday" drift through their lives like sleepwalkers, serving as the perfect mirror to the blank-faced characters that populate the photographs in the *Twilight* series. Even the more emotionally direct songs—"The Crying of Lot G" and "From Black to Blue"— feel like they could take place in Crewdson's eerie suburbs, with the domestic disputes on these tracks carrying an undertone of claustrophobia. The title of "The Crying of Lot G" could even be read as a reflection of these pristine yet anonymous residential areas; the crying, or the argument, could just as easily be taking place in lots A, B, C, or D, for as indistinguishable as they all are.

The other song on *And Then Nothing* with a reference to crying in its title, "Tears Are in Your Eyes," might be its most wounded. On top of a gentle piano and some sliding guitar notes, Georgia tries to convince a depressed friend that things will work out. The song feels equal parts hopeful and despondent, with Georgia switching perspectives on the bridge—adopting the voice of her friend—to question her own assertion that things will be okay. It's another showcase of Yo La Tengo's ability to draw an incredible amount of power from a few simple phrases. It's moving enough when Georgia and Ira's voices come together to sing, "Tears are in your eyes tonight," on the chorus, but it's even more affecting later on in the song when they swap out "tonight" for "every night."

What deepens the song even further is the way it acts as a mirror to the album's most hopeful moment: "Our Way to Fall." There are several lyrical parallels between the two songs: on "Our Way to Fall," Ira sings about staring at his shoes to convey his shyness, and on "Tears Are in Your Eyes," that same image is reused by Georgia to portray him as avoidant instead. The rose-tinted reference to a summer's day that opens "Our Way to Fall" is similarly flipped on its head, with Georgia's character in "Tears Are in Your Eyes" singing, "You tell me summer's here and the time is wrong." The duality between these songs encapsulates that suburban contradiction: from one angle, things appear romantic and pristine, but from another they seem depressingly bleak. These feelings of isolation are also explored in very different ways on *And Then Nothing*'s two most energetic numbers: "Cherry Chapstick" and "Let's Save Tony Orlando's House."

"Cherry Chapstick" is the album's biggest outlier, both sonically and lyrically. Notably, it's one of the few songs on the album not to feature the organ; in fact, there isn't even any bass on it—when the group plays it live, they do so with two electric guitars and a drum set. On an album obsessed with soft, textured landscapes, the song's emphasis on electric guitar thrashing singles it out. It sounds like a group of teenagers having band practice in their parents' garage—and I mean that in the best way possible. Though this heaviness disrupts *And Then Nothing*'s generally serene mood, it does at least feel like a perfect match for the song's lyrics, which, to be honest, call to mind *American Pie* more than *American Beauty*.

"Someone else's date at someone else's door," Ira sings under a haze of distortion, "there's a girl with cherry chapstick on and nothing more." It's as though he's playing the part of a teenage boy from a raunchy late-nineties comedy, pining after the girl next door. The following verses do little to challenge this reading, with Ira going on to sing about swingers and whining that the girls in the neighborhood never check him out. The song ends with him complaining that he's running around in circles, which—intentionally or not—feels like an echo of Crewdson's lawnmower man. Though the lyrics of "Cherry Chapstick" seem ridiculous on the surface, in reality they're mining the same emotional territory as "Everyday" and "Saturday" while wearing a different outfit; the song is about the ennui of being trapped in a routine and the thirst for a more exciting life that comes with that. This is also true of "Let's Save Tony Orlando's House," which, despite its bright and upbeat sound, is concerned with the same restless feelings.

The song originated from a little in-joke among the members of the band. For most of their career, Yo La Tengo have developed new songs by jamming together in their rehearsal space, and it's always been James's job to record these sessions and organize them. Often James will give these songs working titles—little jokes to keep Ira and Georgia entertained—and during the writing of *And Then Nothing*, he decided to name each of the demos after films, shows, and telethons from the extensive resume of Troy McClure, a fictional actor you may remember from *The Simpsons*. This means that, for all we know, the working title for "Last Days of Disco" could've been "Out with Gout '88" or "Astroheist Gemini." Ira was so amused by these demo names that he decided at least one of the songs should retain its original Troy McClure title, and so he penned some lyrics for "Let's Save Tony Orlando's House" based on the song's working title.

The Simpsons reference alone is enough to link the song to *And Then Nothing*'s suburban world—the show is centered around a suburbs-dwelling nuclear family, after all—but when you dig into the actual lyrics of "Let's Save Tony Orlando's House," it's clear the thread runs much deeper. Despite its playful origins, the track contains some of the album's darkest imagery. "Let's Save Tony Orlando's House" centers, as its title suggests, on a fictional fundraising event for the house of Tony Orlando, the seventies pop singer made famous by hits like "Candida" and "Knock Three Times." The opening verse locks in on this image, which sees thousands of people gathering for the fundraiser armed with yellow ribbons, a nudging reference to Orlando's 1973 hit, "Tie a Yellow Ribbon Round the Ole Oak Tree." However, this serene and idyllic atmosphere quickly dissipates when the chorus arrives, shifting the focus to Tony's flame-engulfed home. "Watch it burn," Georgia sings in a serenely detached voice, "acrid smoke makes him wheeze." The deadpan way this undercuts the song's cheerful, charitable opening image calls to mind Lynch's quote about the millions of ants swarming a cherry tree. More than any other song on *And Then Nothing*, "Let's Save Tony Orlando's House" succeeds in holding that light and darkness at the same time. Similar to how *The Virgin Suicides'* warm color palette goes some way to cover up the film's unsettling mood, the song's bright instrumentation—major-key organ notes bathing everything in a sunlit glow—disguises its unsettling imagery. Though Tony is surrounded by a community of supporters on the verses, he's alone on the chorus; it's only him choking on the fumes from the house fire.

The suburbs contradiction—together but alone—at its most extreme.

***

Yo La Tengo's approach to being a band has always involved a similar type of contradiction. Despite getting their start as part of the Hoboken music scene, there are numerous examples of how the band has come to resemble a small, self-sustaining nuclear family. The trio rarely involves other people in their music unless they really have to. "I really think one of our strengths," Ira says, "is that we're very comfortable with each other and much less so with other people."[2]

We only need to examine *Painful*'s liner notes to see this. Other than the members of Yo La Tengo and Roger Moutenot, only three people are credited on the release: Fred Brockman, who assisted with the production; Greg Calibi, who handled the mastering; and Chris Knox, who's responsible for the illustration on the cover. Even more notably, when the time came for the band to record a follow-up, they assembled almost exactly the same lineup to do it. Roger Moutenot and Fred Brockman returned to handle the production and Greg Calibi was once again in charge of the mastering—though this time around Georgia designed the album's cover art. It's also worth pointing out that Roger and his family relocated from New York to Nashville between the recording of these two albums, and Yo La Tengo were so keen to retain the balance they'd found in the *Painful* sessions that they flew out to Tennessee just to work with him again.

You might assume this commitment to stability would cause the band's next album to sound like *Painful Part 2*, but the opposite is true. If anything, it gave them the confidence to grow and experiment further. *Electro-O-Pura* would become the first Yo La Tengo album where every song was credited to the group as a whole, reflecting a shift in their approach to songwriting. Rather than Ira or Georgia bringing an idea for a song to the practice space, which they would then flesh out as a trio, almost all of *Electr-O-Pura*'s tracks were born out of the three band members jamming together. The album is a reflection of just how close Ira, Georgia, and James had gotten. Through relentless touring in support of *Painful*, as well as a rigorous rehearsal schedule, the band members had almost developed a psychic link with each other. As Georgia describes it, the three of them had "joined up as a single-headed monster."[3]

Electr-O-Pura is much more expansive than Yo La Tengo's previous albums. It sees the band twist and distort the sound they'd perfected on *Painful*, digging deeper into their instruments and discovering new ways to bounce off each other. Ira, Georgia, and James were walking a more precarious tightrope than ever before, and Roger, their trusted producer, acted as the essential safety net that stretched out beneath them. His presence led to an environment where experimentation and risk-taking were encouraged. And just as Roger continued to form a key part of the band's recording process, so would their pilgrimages to Nashville. The band's immediate love of the city is reflected in the fact that two of the album's songs—"Flying Lesson (Hot Chicken #1)" and "Don't Say a Word (Hot Chicken #2)"—take their name from a popular food spot in the city: Prince's Hot Chicken Shack. (The opening track from their next album, *I Can Hear the Heart Beating as One*, is also knowingly titled "Return to Hot Chicken.") For as long as Yo La Tengo continued to work with Roger—the next fifteen years—they recorded in Nashville. And that routine gave them the space to grow.

This approach to making music, one in which the band members dig deeper into themselves with every subsequent release rather than reaching outward, reflects how Yo La Tengo continue to operate today. "I think there's certainly an argument to be made that by changing your circumstances, or producers, or backing musicians, it keeps things fresh," Ira muses. "I think we've always approached it the opposite way, that by not changing a lot of things we can build on what we've done."[4]

And *Electr-O-Pura* more than succeeded in building on what the band achieved with *Painful*. Though it's sometimes dismissed as a transitional album—the band's jam-based approach to songwriting would arguably pay off in more rewarding ways on their following records—it remains one of Yo La Tengo's most thrilling releases. *Electr-O-Pura* is held up by the same four instrumental tentpoles as *Painful*—guitar, bass, organ, and drums—but this time there was a willingness to push them to their limits. The gulf between the soft songs and loud ones had never been greater; "False Alarm" drives the cheap Ace Tone Organ sound to its ugly extreme, while "The Hour Grows Late" feels almost hymn-like in its gentleness. *Painful*, despite its varying moods and textures, offered what felt like a unified front, and it's difficult to say the same about *Electr-O-Pura*.

Though not all of the band's experiments succeeded, it's hard to describe anything on *Electr-O-Pura* as boring. "Attack on Love" splits the difference between documentary-sampling ambience and jagged guitar freak-out, while "Decora," colored by tremolo and reversed guitar riffs, boasts a singularly ominous mood. The nine-minute closer "Blue Line Swinger" exists in the same lineage as "Sleeping Pill" and "I Heard You Looking," continuing to chart how impeccably tight the trio were becoming. It still stands as one of Yo La Tengo's most exhilarating moments. Like a storm cloud, the song slowly amasses tension; the instruments emerge one by one—starting with the Ace Tone organ, then Georgia's clattering drums—as the pace gradually begins to pick up. Then, in the final few minutes, all that tension is finally released. Ira, Georgia, and James go all-out on their respective instruments, generating a tornado of noise while remaining perfectly in sync with each other.

In addition to these wilder, boundary-testing moments, *Electr-O-Pura* also features some of Yo La Tengo's most classically catchy songs. "Tom Courtenay," with its sticky guitar hook and Beach Boys-esque backing vocals, sees the band emulate the music of their youth more explicitly than ever before. The accompanying music video, in which the trio opens for a fictional Beatles reunion tour, only underlines its sixties pop sheen further. Then there's the tender and swooning "Pablo and Andrea," which, in its reverb waltz, feels like a prototype for the domestic romances that would later make up much of *And Then Nothing Turned Itself Inside-Out.*

Like *Painful*, *Electr-O-Pura* was warmly received by critics, even if it didn't go on to sell quite as many copies. Robert Christgau of *The Village Voice* gave it an A rating, describing it as "the best record they've ever made,"[5] while in a retrospective review for *Under the Radar*, Ian King described it as "buzz[ing] with the electricity of a band in the whirlwind of new discovery."[6] Despite this warm feedback, what makes *Electr-O-Pura* a great record is the fact that, ultimately, it doesn't seem concerned about what the outside world thinks; the band was slowly ceasing to hold themselves to the wider music industry's definitions of success. "No matter what I'm writing about, I always feel like I'm talking to Georgia and James," Ira says. "If someone else happens to be listening, fine."[7]

As Yo La Tengo's approach to music-making turned more insular, so did the way they handled business matters. Around the time of *Electr-O-Pura*'s 1995 release, the band decided to become self-managed. On the surface, it seems like this move would only draw their attention away from making music, but that didn't happen. Although being self-managed forced the band to sort their own finances and start reading contracts, it also allowed them to remain oblivious to the significant changes the music industry would undergo over the next thirty years. There's something pure about this approach. In a sense, it has allowed the band to remain the same, and operate in the same way, for the majority of their career. To the members of Yo La Tengo, the music is the star of the show—everything else is just set decoration.

***

It's hard not to see the connection shared by Ira, Georgia, and James as the single-most important factor in Yo La Tengo's continued success. During the thirty-plus years that the trio has played together, they've never had any major fallouts. They always move in unison, understanding that their band is the sum of its parts. "Over the years, I've learned that fighting, blowing up, throwing a tantrum, can be fun, yes, but it's a very temporary emotion," Ira says, "which, in reality, only makes things worse."[8] This may be why the group tried to involve as few outsiders as possible when recording *Painful* and *Electr-O-Pura*; they understood the perfect balance they share as a trio is such a rare thing. Why risk throwing it off?

Still, despite the band's unbreakable core, Yo La Tengo have always been indebted to the community that surrounds them. This is traceable back to the Hoboken music scene, which, for a long time, acted as their version of the suburbs. Not the rotting-under-the-surface version that Lynch and Coppola explored in their films, but the idealized, utopian version where everyone supports each other. As shown by the "Big Day Coming" story covered in the last chapter—where Ira and Georgia pushed their way onto the bill of a show at Maxwell's just to try out a new song—Hoboken provided Yo La Tengo with a tight, neighborly community that was committed to helping them flourish. The New York of the eighties was a different beast to the one Ira and Georgia had lived in during the seventies; the city was quickly becoming more gentrified and expensive, making it increasingly difficult for artists like them to survive. Because of this, a counter-community began to form across the Hudson River in the cheaper, rougher Hoboken. When Ira and Georgia first moved there with a couple of friends in the early eighties, they were able to rent a whole house for only $200 a month.

Although Hoboken is technically a city, it didn't feel like one to many of the musicians who relocated there from New York. "Hoboken felt safe and worlds away from Manhattan," remembers Janet Wygal of Hoboken power-pop band the Individuals. "It was kind of like going home to Mom when you're in college."[9] There were no skyscrapers and the mood was distinctly working class. Before Steve Fallon purchased Maxwell's and started putting on shows there, the bar only opened for an hour in the morning and an hour in the evening; it was just somewhere for the dock workers to get a coffee before starting their shift and a beer after they finished it. The relative newness of the Hoboken music scene meant it came with much less baggage. Compared to the New York music scene, where it felt like everyone was competing with each other, the bands in Hoboken were all on the same team. This is reflected, almost literally, in the fact that the members of Yo La Tengo, the dBs, and the Feelies used to play softball together: they all wanted each other to succeed.

The deep network of friends that Yo La Tengo built up through the Hoboken music scene, along with their extensive touring, is arguably the second-most important factor in the band's continued success. The aforementioned "Tom Courtenay" music video exemplifies this well; for as much as the recording of *Electr-O-Pura* was a closed-off process, the "Tom Courtenay" video felt like a celebration of all the relationships Yo La Tengo had formed over the years. From members of Hoboken-based bands—such as Dan Cuddy of the Special Pillow—to local DJs—Tom Scharpling of WFMU—almost everyone that appeared in the video is a friend of the band. Even David Kleiler, director of the "From a Motel 6" video, showed up as a sleazy booking agent.

The group's next music video, for the song "Sugarcube," would be a similarly collaborative effort. For this, the band leveraged their new friendship with comedy duo Bob Odenkirk and David Cross, then known for HBO's *Mr. Show*. Because of this, it resembles a comedy sketch more than an actual music video, with the two comedians cracking jokes over most of the song. In the video, the members of

Yo La Tengo are forced to go to rock school by their record label, where they're taught by Bob and David what it really means to be in a band. The group are given tattoos, taught the best way to trash a hotel room, and made to listen attentively while Bob reads them the lyrics to Rush's "Closer to the Heart." And though *And Then Nothing* didn't receive any music videos, the single art for "You Can Have It All" similarly featured a comedian friend of the band that would go on to become a much bigger star in the following decade: Amy Poehler.

Perhaps the greatest symbol of the community Yo La Tengo have constructed, though, is their annual Hanukkah concerts. Since 2001, the band has performed eight shows for the eight nights of Hanukkah almost every year. These performances originally took place at Maxwell's before moving to the Bowery Ballroom in Manhattan after the venue closed. Although the concerts started off as a way for the group to put on a show for friends during the holiday season while avoiding the cliché of a Christmas party—Ira is Jewish by descent but outspokenly secular in practice— the event quickly snowballed into something much bigger. In addition to Yo La Tengo headlining all eight shows, each night also features a surprise support act and a stand-up performance, as well as a number of special guests. It's impossible to predict who'll show up, with guests over the years including Beach House, Graham Nash, members of Sun Ra Arkestra, comedian Tom Kenny (best known as the voice of SpongeBob), and even Ira's mom.

Throughout all stages of their journey, Yo La Tengo have focused on building connections, even as their songwriting and recording processes remain intensely private. You could argue that, during their early years, this community was crucial to their survival. The majority of those pre-James bassists were simply friends filling in, and it was Maxwell's founder Steve Fallon who, through his label Coyote Records, put out the band's first three albums. This support allowed them to survive and grow at their own pace. It's one of the reasons so few acts have had the same career trajectory as Yo La Tengo; it's very rare for a band to be given that much time and space, to be allowed to take almost a decade to discover their sound. Funnily enough, even Gregory Crewdson was a friend of Georgia and Ira's long before he provided them with the cover for *And Then Nothing Turned Itself Inside-Out*. Prior to achieving success as a photographer, he played guitar in the New York band the Speedies. (They had a minor hit with the song "Let Me Take Your Photo," which feels awfully prophetic given Crewdson's future career.)

This duality has been key to Yo La Tengo's success. As essential as the band's core is—the creative dynamo of Ira, Georgia and James—everything that surrounds them is just as important. They may spend a lot of time alone, in some moments resembling a closed-off family unit, but that doesn't mean they don't talk to their neighbors every single day.

Last Days of Disco

Success in the music industry has always been a tenuous thing. Even if you manage to score a number one hit, or several, there's no guarantee that people will still remember you forty years later. This can be said of Tony Orlando, whose house was on fire in the last chapter; though he generated multiple top ten singles in the mid-seventies—one of them, "Candida," even made it to number one in five countries— he isn't talked about much these days. It's likely that most younger music fans, at least the ones who listen to 25-year-old indie rock, only know him through the Yo La Tengo song named after him, if at all. Another star from the same era, whose career can be retrospectively boiled down to a single hit song, also had a big impact on *And Then Nothing Turned Itself Inside-Out*: George McCrae.

The Florida-born singer started making music in the early sixties with his band, the Jivin' Jets, and then as a duo with his wife, Gwen McCrae, but failed to really break through with either. As the decade wore on and Gwen started to find some success on her own, signing a solo contract with TK Records, George continued to struggle, working as a session singer and occasionally playing club shows in his home city of West Palm Beach. By the early seventies, he was close to hanging up his musical hat and going back to college to study law enforcement. But a chance encounter with Harry Wayne Casey and Richard Finch of soon-to-be disco-funk hitmakers KC and the Sunshine Band changed everything. Casey and Finch had just written an infectious new track called "Rock Your Baby," but Casey didn't have the vocal range to hit the high notes the song needed—so they decided to give it to another artist. For George, it was a case of being in the right place at the right time. Though Casey and Finch had a number of people lined up to give the song a shot, George ended up being the first person to walk into the studio who could reach those high notes.

"Rock Your Baby" was huge. Often celebrated as one of the first hits of the disco era, the 1974 single is credited with laying the groundwork for many of the genre's most enduring songs. ABBA cited it as a key influence for "Dancing Queen," and John Lennon even admitted that it inspired his post-Beatles hit "Whatever Gets You Thru the Night." There's a rickety charm to "Rock Your Baby," almost sounding as though it's held together with duct tape. The stuttering drum machine, the glossy guitar licks, George's tender falsetto—these elements shouldn't fit together as well as they do. While missing the four-to-the-floor oomph of the bigger disco hits that arrived later in the decade, the song has an undeniable groove and charm to it, shown by the fact that it spent two weeks atop the Billboard Hot 100 and three weeks at number one in the UK. After the single blew up, George and company quickly followed it up with an album, also called *Rock Your Baby*. Though George would never soar as high as he did on

"Rock Your Baby" again, the album did end up spawning some additional minor hits, including the peppy "I Can't Leave You Alone" and a bouncing number called "You Can Have It All."

Yo La Tengo and George McCrae exist in different universes. While the early trajectory of their careers match up pretty well—a decade's worth of work before that first proper breakthrough—McCrae is maybe the last act you'd expect Yo La Tengo to cover in the year 2000. Even more so, you wouldn't expect that cover to turn into one of the band's most enduring songs. But the trio's ability to take an old, obscure disco number and truly make it their own tells us a lot about their continued success as a band.

Although Yo La Tengo's version of "You Can Have It All" mostly sheds the disco sheen of the original, it retains its DIY aesthetic. Like McCrae's version, Yo La Tengo's is built around a shuffling drum machine beat—the same Casio that colors much of *And Then Nothing*—and the steady hum of an organ. Their version of the song somehow succeeds in sounding both playfully goofy and achingly sincere at the same time; goofy because of Ira and James's wordless bop-bop backing vocals—during live performances they often provide synchronized dance moves as well—and sincere because of Georgia's pure, direct delivery of the song's lyrics. Whereas McCrae's version sounds larger than life thanks to his superhuman falsetto, Yo La Tengo's sounds undeniably human. There's a karaoke-like quality to it in the best possible sense, as if Georgia is standing in her living room, serenading someone she loves with a song that's familiar to them.

Perhaps the biggest issue with McCrae's version is that it sounds like a product of its time. It was written to fit into the existing musical landscape, one where disco was on the rise. After "Rock Your Baby" became a hit and McCrae found himself with an unexpected music career, it made sense to get an album out as quickly as possible to capitalize on that success. This is why many of the songs on *Rock Your Baby* feel half-baked and dated; most of them, including "You Can Have It All," were simply quick attempts from McCrae, Casey, and Finch to replicate the magic of that first single. In comparison, the Yo La Tengo version sounds timeless. It doesn't belong to 2000, 1974, or any other year. That blend between goofiness and sincerity feels true to who Yo La Tengo are as people.

***

Ultimately, *Rock Your Baby* ended up being George McCrae's only album to crack the Billboard chart—reaching a respectable thirty-eight—though he continued to release new music throughout the decade, including two more albums the following year. This isn't a unique story though; as big as disco was in the mid-seventies, only a small handful of acts managed to have any real lasting power—Donna Summers, the Bee Gees, Chic, ABBA—and the same can be said for every other significant music trend that has come and gone since then. For every act that endures, there are hundreds, if not thousands, who don't.

When Ira and Georgia first started making music in the mid-eighties, they often found themselves lumped in with the other college-rock acts that emerged around the same time. For a while they were seen as an imitation of fellow Hobokenites the Feelies. The band's 1980 debut *Crazy Rhythms* had been a critical hit—landing at seventeen on *The Village Voice*'s Pazz & Jop poll for that year—and given that there were so few Hoboken bands breaking through at the time, it's not hard to see why critics used them as a benchmark for assessing Yo La Tengo's first few albums. Still, the Feelies themselves were a small fish in a big pond; while many college-rock acts achieved substantial success during the eighties, only a small handful managed to translate that momentum into a long-term career. For every U2 or Pixies, there are a dozen artists forgotten. To achieve lasting success, it was necessary for bands to grow and evolve; if they didn't want to end up on a "We Love the Eighties" nostalgia tour twenty years later, they needed to prove they were bigger than the decade and genre they were originally associated with.

Out of all the acts that rose out of the eighties college-rock scene, R.E.M.'s career is often held up as an ideal. Their steady trajectory as a band and commitment to constant reinvention can almost be seen as a blueprint for what Yo La Tengo would go on to achieve. After releasing a string of acclaimed jangly rock albums in the eighties, R.E.M. retooled their sound to be quieter and more introspective at the beginning of the nineties, with lead singer Michael Stipe shifting from wordless mumblings to expressive croonings on singles like "Losing My Religion" and "Everybody Hurts." Then, after their most somber album, *Automatic for the People*, managed to shift almost two million copies in the United States, they followed it up with one that went in the complete opposite direction: *Monster*.

On it, R.E.M. eschewed their early nineties sound almost completely and pivoted into the world of glam rock, all while topping the US albums chart once again.

Although Yo La Tengo haven't succeeded on the same commercial scale as R.E.M., their interest in continually reconfiguring their sound is comparable. While a number of different genre labels have been affixed to the band over the years—indie rock, shoegaze, folk, noise pop, dream pop—they've always refused to fit into one box tidily. A brief glance at the most popular Yo La Tengo songs on streaming platforms only seems to confirm this. Their most played song on Spotify is "I'll Be Around," a tender finger-picked ballad from 2013's *Fade*. This is followed by "Autumn Sweater." The complete opposite of "I'll Be Around" instrumentally speaking, it features no guitars at all, only two drum sets, some bongos, and an organ. Next is "You Can Have It All," which, as we've discussed, mutates a forgotten seventies disco hit. Fourth on the list? "Green Arrow," an ambient slide guitar track that samples the air conditioner in the band's practice space. Yo La Tengo have succeeded in transcending genre and decade labels because they're always trying to reinvent themselves, often doing so in several different ways in the span of a single album. This is the reason why audiences at their shows span as many decades as their own career; some fans have been with the band since *Painful*, while others may have come onboard after hearing the ambient murmurings of 2018's *There's a Riot Going On*.

By the time of *Electr-O-Pura*'s release in 1995, the musical landscape around Yo La Tengo had reshaped itself multiple times. Many of the college-rock acts that the band had toured alongside in the eighties had already disappeared—even the Feelies broke up in 1992—and the alternative rock scene that Nirvana ushered in around the time of *May I Sing with Me*'s release was beginning to collapse in on itself. There's no greater symbol of how disparate the music scene was in 1995 than that year's Lollapalooza, which saw Yo La Tengo play alongside—or in truth, at the bottom of the bill of—a wild assortment of acts including Hole, Cypress Hill, Sonic Youth, Sinead O'Connor, Pavement, and Moby. In their retrospective on Lollapalooza 1995, *The Washington Post* described that year's festival as "alternative nation's last stand,"[1] the moment before the heaviness of grunge bands like Pearl Jam, Smashing Pumpkins, and Hole gave way completely to more radio-friendly rock acts like Third Eye Blind and Matchbox Twenty.

Lollapalooza's 1995 installment was infamously rife with drama. Though Sonic Youth were booked as the headliner, Hole frontwoman Courtney Love ended up soaking up most of the spotlight, partly due to the recency of Kurt Cobain's suicide. (Sonic Youth's Lee Ranaldo speculated that a lot of people turned up to the festival just hoping to see some sort of meltdown from her.[2]) Despite this, apart from the occasional table tennis match against the members of Pavement, Yo La Tengo mostly kept to themselves. More than any of the feuds and conflicts that took place at the traveling festival, the trio would remember Lollapalooza for the excruciating heatwave that colored most of it. "It was sort of horrible," Ira recalls, "but really fun in that way of like, 'I'm climbing Mount Everest.'"[3]

The band's placement at the bottom of the Lollapalooza lineup can be read as a metaphor for Yo La Tengo's position in the wider music landscape of the nineties and early 2000s: beyond the Maxwell's community they had risen out of, the band didn't really belong to any scene—the closest they came to being associated with grunge was once allowing Mudhoney to sleep on their couch. Not that this stopped people from trying to find a label for them. During one interview around the time of *And Then Nothing*'s release, Ira was asked whether Yo La Tengo considered itself part of the growing slowcore scene, which included acts like Low, Tram, and Red House Painters. "I have to say I don't know any of those groups you've named," Ira responded. "I think that when we feel like part of a scene, it's usually more social than anything else. I guess that lets us maybe be a little more eclectic musically, but still feel socially tied in with people."[4] This feels very much in line with what we explored in the last chapter: Yo La Tengo were a part of the Hoboken music scene, yes, but not necessarily from a musical perspective. When they involved members of other bands in their music during those early years, such as the many people who filled in on bass, it was a social move more than a musical one. They were simply asking their friends for help.

Yo La Tengo have never felt particularly tied to any music scene because they've never sounded like they're in conversation with what their contemporaries are doing. The band members are always pulling from a number of different places sonically, as demonstrated by their relationship with cover songs. Even before Ira and Georgia formed Yo La Tengo, they'd already learned how to play hundreds of different covers through their prior group, Georgia & Those Guys, due to the fact that the band had a rule they could only play each song live once. By the mid-nineties they had more songs under their belt than a seasoned wedding band. While touring behind *Electr-O-Pura*, Yo La Tengo covered everyone from Blondie to Gram Parsons and Quincy Jones at their shows. If we are to view the band's covers repertoire as a reflection of what they were listening to, then it's easy to see why their own music doesn't feel particularly tied to a specific decade or scene; artists from the sixties, seventies, eighties, and nineties are all feeding into their sound, so how can they be expected to resemble any of their contemporaries?

Ira, Georgia, and James's omnivorous listening habits would rear their head more than ever on their next release, *I Can Hear the Heart Beating as One*. Listening to the album, it would be difficult to tie Yo La Tengo directly to any active music scene from 1997, whether that be alternative rock, folk, slowcore, or something else entirely.

I Can Hear took the experimentation first seen on *Electr-O-Pura* and dialed it up to eleven. The first Yo La Tengo album to clock in at over an hour, it saw the band dabble in a dozen different genres across its sixteen tracks. This was partly possible due to the increased variety of instruments used; while Yo La Tengo mainly stuck to their core instrumental palette on *Electr-O-Pura*, here, for the first time since *Fakebook*, the group invited outside musicians to add additional touches to some of the songs. Al Perkins added lap steel and pedal steel to two tracks, "Moby Octopad" and "One PM Again," and Jonathan Marx brought some trumpet flourishes to "Shadows," while producer Roger Moutenot reportedly played the bongos on "Autumn Sweater." Not only that, but the core trio started integrating new sonic textures by themselves, including a sample of composer Burt Bacharach's "Bird Bath" ("Moby Octopad") and a tinny samba beat sourced from their Casio keyboard's built-in drum machine ("Center of Gravity"). James also took on lead vocal duties for the first time as well with the Neil Young-tinged "Stockholm Syndrome."

While the album features some of the group's most classically Yo La Tengo songs—the distortion-frazzled "Sugarcube" remains the most straightforward rocker they've ever recorded—*I Can Hear* is best loved for its unexpected genre detours. No two songs sound the same. It's like an old patchwork blanket: a medley of clashing materials stitched together that somehow manage to complement each other. Starting with the borderline ambient opener, "Return to Hot Chicken," the band quickly gets to work reshaping people's understanding of what Yo La Tengo sound like. There's the kitschy pop charm of "My Little Corner of the World" (a cover of Anita Bryant's 1960 original), the serene field-recording ambience of "Green Arrow," the bossa-nova two-step of "Center of Gravity," and, on the album's longest track—the almost eleven-minute "Spec Bebop"—the group even investigates krautrock and drone. As well as building on the sounds explored on *Electr-O-Pura*, *I Can Hear the Heart Beating as One* feels like an attempt to compress Ira, Georgia, and James's record collections down into the runtime of a single CD. Heck, there's even a Beach Boys cover.

For most of the songs on *I Can Hear*, Yo La Tengo's points of influence are easy to pick out. Occasionally though, the group drew inspiration from unexpected places, such as on the album's penultimate track, "We're an American Band."

During the tour for *Electr-O-Pura*, the band had started covering the Grand Funk Railroad song of the same name; the song's lyrics felt so at odds with who Yo La Tengo were—focused on topics such as partying, tearing up hotel rooms, and sleeping with groupies—that Ira thought it'd be funny to end their sets with it. Then they decided it'd be an even better idea to write a song with the same title. Musically, the song has little in common with the original "We're an American Band," and lyrically even less. In the verses, Ira sings about playing his favorite Hootie & The Blowfish song in the car and trying to decide which film to see at the cinema. It's silly, but it also drives home a clear message: even though Yo La Tengo aren't trashing hotel rooms and doing other typical rock star stuff, that doesn't mean they're any less an American band than Grand Funk Railroad. In fact, the way they behave, like ordinary people writing songs about ordinary feelings, arguably makes them an even truer type of American band.

Reflective of this, *I Can Hear the Heart Beating as One* planted Yo La Tengo in the American public's consciousness more than any of their previous releases. The album went on to shift over 300,000 copies in the United States and helped the band fill bigger venues than they ever had before. *I Can Hear* was also a huge critical smash as well, ranking high on a number of year-end and decade-end lists, and retrospectively is seen as the group's career album. For as much as Yo La Tengo strives to be a band that never looks back, even they have acknowledged the album's importance in their discography. "If we're at the merch table and someone's asking, 'I don't have any of your records, which one should we get?' we know this one's the answer," Ira says.[5]

If you were to attach a genre label to *I Can Hear*, the most fitting one would be pop. While it might not be pop music in the sense of what was topping the charts in the late nineties—nothing on here sounds like Madonna or Britney Spears—it represents that genre in the most timeless way. Pop in the sense that the feelings it explores are huge and relatable.

***

The sound of *And Then Nothing Turned Itself Inside-Out* is more unified than *I Can Hear the Heart Beating as One*, but that doesn't mean Yo La Tengo's incorporation of their influences into it is any less creative. In fact, I'd argue that the album features some of the band's boldest interpretations of other people's music. You only need to look at "You Can Have It All" to see this; not only did the band draw inspiration from an incredibly unlikely source, but they transformed the song to the point where it sounded completely unrecognizable, translating it into their distinct musical language.

Another track where Yo La Tengo does this is "Last Days of Disco." Discussing the song's origins, Ira cited an unexpected source of inspiration for its lyrics: Kool & The Gang's 1980 hit, and eternal birthday party playlist mainstay, "Celebration." "They say, 'Celebrate!' and most of the time you just kind of roll your eyes at it," Ira says of the song's sentiment. "And then, one night, they say, 'Celebrate!' and you celebrate."[6] In the lyrics of "Last Days of Disco," we see the protagonist attempt to give himself over to the dance floor, while also trying to ignore the niggly fears in the back of his head, like the fact that he isn't wearing the right clothes for dancing. Eventually though, the music hits him in the right way and he finally understands what it's all about; the song tells him to be happy and suddenly he's happy. What makes the link between "Celebration" and "Last Days of Disco" so interesting is that the two songs couldn't sound less alike. In comparison to "Celebration," an aggressively upbeat disco stomper with a singalong chorus, "Last Days of Disco" is quietly introverted. The instrumentation is muted and woozy; guitar notes and snare hits skitter off into the distance like shy teens leaving a school dance early. Similarly, rather than yelling the song's lyrics to a packed-out room, it sounds as though Ira is gently murmuring them to himself.

"Tired Hippo," the penultimate song on *And Then Nothing*, is another classic Yo La Tengo transformation. Built around a playful drum-machine beat and the drone of an organ, it's the most skeletal track on the album and the only one not to feature lyrics. To my ears, it almost sounds like the band's attempt at writing the theme for a spy thriller; there's something distinctly James Bond about the way the song slinks along. And yet, at the same time, it remains unmistakably Yo La Tengo. Just like "You Can Have It All," there's something lightly goofy about the burping drum machine that calls to mind the personalities of Ira, Georgia, and James.

And Then Nothing also pulls from a wider range of sources than *I Can Hear*. In addition to the obvious musical influences that pop up across the album—"Madeline" sounds like a lost sixties-pop ditty while "Cherry Chapstick" owes a lot to old-school garage rock—the band also reference other art forms. Besides Gregory Crewdson's photography, you can spot references to several books, TV shows, and films.

It's there in the song names: "Last Days of Disco" takes its title from the 1998 Whit Stillman film of the same name, "The Crying of Lot G" references Thomas Pynchon's novel *The Crying of Lot 69*, and, as we've discussed, "Let's Save Tony Orlando's House" owes its origins to a joke from *The Simpsons*. The media they draw inspiration from never feels highbrow, but instead everyday; the cultural figures that pop up in *And Then Nothing*'s lyrics range from *American Graffiti* star Paul Le Matt to model Kate Moss. When asked about the number of cultural references on the album, Ira responded in a typically Ira way: "They're just part of my life and they're not anything to run away from or to hide."[7]

Unlike some of the larger-than-life characters that Yo La Tengo toured alongside as part of Lollapalooza, Ira, Georgia, and James have always felt like ordinary Americans. And through its blend of pop culture references, unexpected musical influences, and aching sincerity, *And Then Nothing Turned Itself Inside-Out* feels like the truest display of who they are. Rather than changing themselves to fit a specific mold, projecting the stereotypical image of an American band like, say, Grand Funk Railroad, they've always asked their audience to accept them for who they are. As Roger Moutenot describes it, "If you understand Yo La Tengo, this is their life. This is what they've given their life to: this band, making music."[8]

Although Yo La Tengo never achieved the same level of success as R.E.M., perhaps that was a good thing. While R.E.M. was still chasing hits later in their career, it ultimately ended up damaging them slightly. Their success in the nineties, as seismic as it was, acted as a benchmark that they continued to measure their career against in later decades. To "succeed," for them, was to achieve success on that same scale again. Through having had a much more modest definition of success—making music purely for themselves and not worrying about who's going to listen to it—Yo La Tengo have managed to maintain a respectable career. Even if *I Can Hear the Heart Beating as One* is seen as their career album, it's not like their popularity dropped off significantly after it; instead, their career has continued at the same steady level in the decades since. As other acts rise and fall, Yo La Tengo remains a constant.

Nothing Turned Itself Inside Out …

If Lollapalooza 1995 is often characterized as alternative rock's last stand, then by 1998 the genre was well and truly dead. Following an underwhelming turnout for the 1996 and 1997 installments, and after failing to find a suitable headliner for 1998, the festival went on an extended hiatus, only returning in 2003 when co-founder Perry Farrell revived his own band, Jane's Addiction, to headline it. "Lollapalooza is as comatose as alternative rock is right now," *Spin* declared in a 1998 issue.[1] And, as if to drive the point home further, that same issue also featured Dave Matthews on the cover, accompanied by a headline declaring him "the king of rock."[2]

Still, even if the scene Yo La Tengo regularly found themselves associated with was in serious decline, the band's own career was moving in an upward trajectory. Fresh off the release of *I Can Hear the Heart Beating as One*, Ira, Georgia, and James were bigger than ever. Their eighth album received universal praise upon its release and quickly outpaced the group's previous records in terms of sales. Given this increased exposure, the tour behind *I Can Hear* was fittingly exhaustive; the band embarked on two extensive US legs as well as multiple trips to Europe in 1997 alone. In early 1998, the group also played to audiences in Australia and New Zealand for the first time. Now thirteen years deep into their career, it seemed like the trio's hard work was finally paying off in a significant way.

For a band that had spent most of its career referencing pop culture in its music, Yo La Tengo was also beginning to become a cultural force of its own. Opportunities were coming in left, right and center, with gigantic brands such as Coca-Cola, Starbucks, and NASCAR all requesting the band's songs for their commercials. However, in typical Yo La Tengo fashion, they made the decision not to allow their existing songs to be used in advertisements; instead, the group countered specific song requests by offering to write new ones in the same style. Though the band did end up losing some business by taking this stance, many brands agreed to their terms, as shown by the Yo La Tengo-soundtracked Coca-Cola commercial that aired during the 1996 Summer Olympics. The trio also found themselves producing music for film and TV, scoring two Hal Hartley films—*Simple Men* and *The Book of Life*—as well as recording a psychedelic cover of *The Simpsons* theme for the 1998 episode "D'Oh in the Wind." In early 2000, the producers of *Gilmore Girls* asked if they could use Yo La Tengo's version of "My Little Corner of the World" for the closing credits of the show's pilot episode. Though the group declined, they'd eventually end up guest-starring on the show a few years later after James became a fan.

The way the band members have characterized this success varies. While Georgia has noted that she found the group's increased visibility slightly overwhelming,[3] Ira's reaction was more joking. "It's funny," he says, "because bands get really popular and we only got a little more popular."[4] Still, popularity is relative, and it's likely that Ira and Georgia never expected to get as far as they had when they first started playing covers at Maxwell's back in 1983. And although Yo La Tengo were treated as a budget version of the Feelies in those early days, they were now pulling much bigger crowds than their fellow Hobokenites ever had. For all the groups that Ira and Georgia had come up alongside in the city—the Bongos, the dBs, the Individuals—Yo La Tengo were seen as the definitive Hoboken band by the end of the nineties. And it was something they'd managed without ever having to compromise who they were or what type of music they wanted to make. They'd achieved it all on their own terms.

***

After spending the best part of two years playing shows in support of *I Can Hear the Heart Beating as One*, the trio was finally able to retreat home at the end of 1998. Given the globe-trotting scope of the tour, it likely felt good to be back in Hoboken with its clear, stable confines. Things in Yo La Tengo's home city had changed though; the building that housed the band's rehearsal space had been scheduled for demolition after the owner had decided to sell it to condo developers, meaning they needed to find somewhere new to practice. The place they landed on was situated in a run-down industrial estate just outside of Jersey City, a notable shift from the old spot nestled in the heart of Hoboken. Just as the songs that made up *Electr-O-Pura* and *I Can Hear* were born out of the three members jamming in their old practice space, the songs on *And Then Nothing* came from them jamming in their new one, and it's likely that this shift in location had a big impact on the types of songs they started writing. Certain things just sounded better there. "It was never part of the plan to make a quiet record," Ira notes. "It seemed to keep happening that when we'd play loud it just wasn't sticking, if we played quiet, it was."[5]

Yo La Tengo have always remained intensely private about the behind-the-scenes aspects of their music. When promoting the 2013 reissue of *Painful*, Ira made sure to express his reluctance at explaining what the songs were about and how the band had written them. "I think the record having its own mysteries is a good thing," he says. "I understand the impulse to have the questions answered, but I'm not sure as listeners we weren't better off with the questions."[6] The making of every Yo La Tengo album is characterized as an unconscious process by the three members of the band—a type of psychic link-up between Ira, Georgia, and James and their instruments. They never approach an album with a particular sound or theme in mind; they just start playing together and see what emerges.

Still, every Yo La Tengo album draws heavily on the experiences of the band's three members. There are infinite examples of this across *I Can Hear*'s tracklist alone: "Green Arrow" was inspired by the sound of the air conditioner in the band's practice space, while the title of "Moby Octopad" originated from their time on the Lollapalooza tour, where they frequently shared a stage with Moby and his Roland Octopad. As a result, it's not a leap to assume that the overall sound of *And Then Nothing*, subconsciously or not, was the group's way of reacting to the unexpected success of their previous album. Although *I Can Hear* did feature some of Yo La Tengo's most demanding songs to date—like the odyssean "Spec Bebop"—overall, the album was much more accessible than anything the group had previously released. You only need to hear a song like "Autumn Sweater" or "Damage" once to connect with it. There's something classically pop about the majority of the album's songs, even if many of them are wearing vastly different genre outfits.

Most of the songs that emerged from the first jam sessions for *And Then Nothing* felt less obvious though. The music that sounded best in the group's new rehearsal space was decidedly darker and slower than anything they'd produced before. One of the first songs the band debuted from the album, during a 1998 Peel Session, was "Tired Hippo." Compared to the bright, technicolor tone of the songs on *I Can Hear*, "Tired Hippo" feels downright skeletal. The song doesn't feature a big chorus or, well, any chorus at all; there aren't even any lyrics. It's about as far away from "Autumn Sweater" and "Sugarcube" as the band could possibly get. It's as though the trio wanted to make a record that people would find impossible to compare directly with *I Can Hear*, which, by the time of *And Then Nothing*'s release, was already being celebrated as one of the best albums of the nineties. Yo La Tengo had set a high benchmark for themselves and so the only logical way to move their career forward—and not be seen as a band in decline—was to produce something radically and incomparably different. You only need to compare the covers of the two albums to understand how dissimilar they are; while *I Can Hear*'s features New York City in the daytime, decorated brightly with gold, red, and pink, *And Then Nothing*'s depicts a sleepy suburban home in the blue-toned dead of night. The difference between them is, literally, night and day.

No instrument highlights the yin-yang relationship between these two albums better than the band's Casio drum machine. First deployed on "Center of Gravity," one of *I Can Hear*'s most infectiously catchy songs, the instrument crops up frequently across *And Then Nothing* to achieve a very different effect. "Saturday," as we've already explored, is one of the album's bleakest and most dissociative moments, exploring the malaise of a weekend in which nothing noteworthy happens. Although the information-overload presentation of the song is key to its dissonant mood—with the band piling a dozen different instruments into it, including keyboards, shakers, wind chimes, and a harmonica—the rattling drum machine serves as its restless core. It's the train track that all the other instruments are trundling along. While the drum machine on "Center of Gravity" can be described as charmingly peppy, the one on "Saturday" feels distorted and unsettled; fed through delay and reverb pedals, it swerves and twists back on itself. It's as though that train track is leading us off the edge of a cliff.

According to Georgia, many of the songs the band wrote for *And Then Nothing* emerged from drum loops. All three members would take turns behind the kit, playing for a couple of minutes alongside a beat from the Casio machine. They would then stretch these loops out and jam on top of them. You can feel this when listening to the album. Although less than half of *And Then Nothing*'s songs ended up featuring a drum machine—"You Can Have It All," "Madeline," "Tired Hippo," "Everyday," and "Saturday"—the instrument's icy mood emanates through the whole record. The drum machine's rigidity reflects many of the album's themes, like the dullness of routine and the isolation of the suburbs, giving it enough presence to bleed into songs that feature more traditional drums, like "Tears Are in Your Eyes." It's similar to how the Ace Tone Organ feels representative of *Painful*'s sound as a whole, despite not appearing on every song.

This embrace of the drum machine is also another example of Yo La Tengo's intuition-led approach to making music, and their insistence on marching to the beat of their own (digital) drum. In addition to their trusty Casio, the band made extensive use of an Ace Tone Rhythm Ace, a drum machine best known for its use on seventies albums like J.J. Cale's self-titled debut and Sly & The Family Stone's *There's a Riot Goin' On*. There was a certain irony to Yo La Tengo's embrace of these outdated, untrendy instruments at a time when electronica artists like the Chemical Brothers and the Prodigy were becoming the new rock stars. "Everyone was into drum 'n' bass and samplers," James says, "and I was so excited that our version of that was, 'Hey, what does the Casio drum machine sound like?'"[7] Whereas many bands were trying to predict what the new millennium would sound like—Radiohead's *Kid A* was released the same year—Yo La Tengo were almost looking backward.

Another instrument that crops up frequently across *And Then Nothing* is the vibraphone. Just like the Ace Tone Rhythm Ace, hardly anyone was using it anymore by the late nineties. It was an instrument best known for its use on sixties pop albums like the Beach Boys' *Pet Sounds* and the Supremes' *Where Did Our Love Go*. But, as with every other instrument Yo La Tengo have integrated into their sound over the years, they didn't approach it through the lens of whether it was current or not; instead, just like the guitar, drums or organ, they simply saw it as another way to express themselves. Georgia apparently stumbled upon the instrument by accident, lying around the Nashville studio where they were recording *And Then Nothing*. She'd never tried playing one before but immediately decided to add some vibraphone to "Our Way to Fall"—and it's that first take, her first attempt at playing it, that ultimately ended up on the final album. Remembering this moment, Roger Moutenot says, "Georgia doesn't play vibes, but there's something beautiful about that. You don't have this guy that's just flowery on the vibes, you've got Georgia and she's just reaching for that C and is just an 8th note behind. And that's character and I love that."[8] Georgia's lack of proficiency on the vibraphone adds something to "Our Way to Fall" that no professional player would be able to. Her hesitant, slightly off playing style feels like a perfect reflection of the vulnerability conveyed by the lyrics. And this inquisitive approach to making music is one of the things that has come to define Yo La Tengo. For as long as they've been going, and for as much music as they've released, the trio always come across as real people first and professional musicians second. The way they use their instruments always feels like an attempt to express feelings that are impossible to get across with words alone.

The finest example of Yo La Tengo's intuition-based approach to songwriting comes with the album's final track, "Night Falls on Hoboken." Although many of *And Then Nothing*'s songs were born out of extended percussive loops, this is the one moment on the final album where the band really let things sprawl out. At eighteen minutes long—one whole side on the LP version—the song seems to contain an entire universe. It's a tone poem that stretches on endlessly, moving through several phases during its runtime, proving that Yo La Tengo are just as good at speaking with their instruments as they are with their voices.

Whereas previous Yo La Tengo albums climaxed with guitar heroics—"I Heard You Looking," "Blue Line Swinger," "We're An American Band"—*And Then Nothing*'s closing track is a long slow drift. Patient, textured, and gently ominous, "Night Falls on Hoboken" feels like the perfect culmination of everything that came before it. *And Then Nothing* has always been an album that invites night-time metaphors, and though it is by no means a concept album, it does at times feel like the band is telling us the story of one lengthy night, from the anxious dance floor strutting of "Last Days of Disco" to the hushed kitchen argument that takes place in "The Crying of Lot G." Following this extended metaphor, "Night Falls on Hoboken" represents the moment after the main character crawls into bed and, trying to quiet the worries in their head, hopelessly yearns for sleep.

Like most of the songs on the album, "Night Falls on Hoboken" was born in the band's practice space. For a long time, only the first few minutes of the song existed—the part of the final track that contains vocals—until one day, when rehearsing it, the band decided to just keep going. The song quickly evolved from a simple acoustic strummer into something much more sprawling in scope, shifting through several phases and moods, and requiring Ira and James to swap to different instruments partway through. According to Ira, the song didn't evolve much after they played the long version for the first time; it's as though they were just channeling something, moving in unison without really thinking about it.

For its first few minutes, though, "Night Falls on Hoboken" is simple and sparse. The trio maintains a steady, repetitive loop on their respective instruments while Ira and Georgia softly croon the song's despondent lyrics. "Come on, let's leave our misery," the chorus goes, "and crawl towards where we want to be." It feels not only like a hint toward the song's slow, three-chord crawl, but also an echo of the themes explored on songs like "Saturday" and "Tears Are in Your Eyes"— that desire to keep moving forward, even when things are at their most hopeless. This is another way that "Night Falls on Hoboken" differs from the band's previous album closers; while there is a hint of hopefulness to the song's lyrics, they don't provide the clear sense of catharsis you'd expect from the end of an album. To be honest, it sounds as though they've ended up in the exact place they were at its beginning. Things just continue on, the everyday repeating itself.

After those first five minutes, which follow a typical verse-chorus structure, the song's restlessness intensifies. While James and Georgia stick to the same steady rhythm on their instruments, Ira begins to manipulate his guitar, looping riffs, driving up the feedback, and distorting it to sound like several different things. At one point it resembles a trapped fly, buzzing around the room and throwing itself against a closed window, and at another it sounds like a series of cars rushing by on the road outside. All of this contributes to the feeling of lying awake at night, trying to drift off, even as the world around you refuses to allow it. Then, once he's wrangled everything he can out of his guitar, Ira moves over to a second drum set and starts bashing away, while James swaps to the Ace Tone. Eventually the warm, glittering tone of the organ washes over everything, smothering Ira's leftover guitar loops. And finally, the song is allowed to fade into dreamless sleep.

In an interview with *The Guardian*, James compared the recording process for "Night Falls on Hoboken" to "an elaborate tracking shot in a movie."[9] Due to the trio's insistence that it all be recorded in one take without any overdubs, the studio had to be laid out in a very precise manner. Not only did the band members need to be able to swap instruments easily partway through the song, but the amps needed to be set up in such a way that Ira could easily control the level of feedback on his guitar. In the end, guitar amps were set up in the corridor outside of the studio, and then, following the initial distortion-free opening of the song, Roger opened the door for Ira so he could head outside and start generating feedback. Issues also sprung up from the fact that the song started incredibly quiet before slowly growing louder, meaning that Ira had to take off his headphones partway through the song to avoid blowing out his ears. "Every time we'd solve one problem, it'd cause another one," he recalls. "And I think it did take us an entire day to come up with a strategy for how we could play that song for seventeen minutes. And then that's what we did the next day."[10]

Yo La Tengo's insistence on doing things their own way ended up paying off. The making of "Night Falls on Hoboken" encapsulates their philosophy as a band: they could've taken an easier or more obvious path when it came to following up *I Can Hear the Heart Beating as One*, yes, but that wouldn't have felt true to who Ira, Georgia, and James are. In that sense, *And Then Nothing Turned Itself Inside-Out* feels like art in the most honest, most human way. They went into their practice space with nothing and slowly turned it into something.

… And Became Something

The particular way *And Then Nothing Turned Itself Inside-Out* emerged into the world echoes the album's sonic identity. Whereas *I Can Hear the Heart Beating as One* was released in spring, representative of its warm, kaleidoscopic mood, *And Then Nothing* was released at the tail end of winter, on February 22, 2000, a time of year when the days are short and the nights long. The way the band promoted the record was similarly nocturnal, demonstrated by the choice of "Saturday" as a lead single. Rather than introducing people to the album with one of its more accessible moments—like "You Can Have It All," "Let's Save Tony Orlando's House," or even "Our Way to Fall"—the decision to go with "Saturday" suggests Yo La Tengo wanted listeners to know *And Then Nothing* would be moodier and less immediate than their previous releases. There was no "Autumn Sweater" this time around.

This single choice also feels representative of where the music industry was in 2000, as well as Yo La Tengo's place in it. In the broadest financial sense, things had never been better; according to the Recording Industry Association of America (RIAA), US music sales hit their all-time high in

1999,[1] with CD sales peaking in 2000.[2] The rise of CDs during the nineties had helped labels generate higher profits than ever before, mostly thanks to the huge margins on them— the average CD retailed for $14, despite costing less than $2 to produce[3]—and because the new format allowed them to resell older artists' catalogues to consumers for a second or third time after the previous waves of vinyl and cassettes. As a knock-on effect of this financial golden age, major labels were able to make investments in artists they probably wouldn't have in the eighties, demonstrated by Atlantic Records' decision to partner with Matador in 1993. It's hard to imagine an album like *Painful* receiving a big push from a major label in any other decade, or a music video as tongue-in-cheek as "Sugarcube" getting any airtime on MTV. And while Yo La Tengo did their best to remain independent from everything else happening in the nineties alternative scene, it's debatable whether they would have been able to flourish in the way they did if the music landscape wasn't at such a ridiculous financial peak. Combined with their unmatched work ethic, it acted as the launchpad their career needed.

However, by the time *And Then Nothing* was released, the tides were slowly beginning to shift. Even if 1999 was objectively the best year for music sales since the RIAA started tracking them, cracks were already beginning to appear. In 1996, the first illegal MP3 rip was shared online— Metallica's "Until It Sleeps"[4]—and though the majority of American households wouldn't own a computer that could connect to the internet until the early 2000s, people quickly saw the potential of this new file format. Two of these people, Shawn Fanning and Sean Parker, ended up founding the peer-to-peer file sharing application Napster in 1999, and the impact that it and similar platforms had on the industry was seismic. Although yearly music sales hit their peak of $23.7 billion in 1999, by 2014, a mere fifteen years later, they would hit a low of $7.7 billion.[5] The numbers have improved in the years since, thanks to the rise of streaming platforms, but it's unlikely that the industry will ever come anywhere close to those profit highs of the nineties again, and a much smaller piece of the pie seems to go to the artists.

Even before music piracy had done any significant damage to the industry, the way some artists and labels responded to it foreshadowed how things would play out. The most infamous example is Metallica, who, in the same year that *And Then Nothing* was released, tried to sue Napster for $10 million after discovering users were sharing their songs on the platform for free.[6] As you'd expect, this move ended up backfiring on the band; not only did the lawsuit provide Napster with free publicity, causing more users to flock to the platform than ever before, it also made Metallica look like they were declaring war on their fans. How were people supposed to feel sorry for a band like Metallica or their label Elektra when, as mentioned, they were raking in a $12 profit on every $2 CD they produced?

All this to say that *And Then Nothing* and its early 2000 release date seemed to straddle two very distinct eras for the music industry: one of substantial growth and one of equally substantial decline. The way that Yo La Tengo and Matador Records navigated this shift feels incredibly important when talking about the band's continued relevance. It encapsulates how they've managed to stay successful and maintain such a passionate following over the two decades since that record's release.

You could describe Yo La Tengo's response to music piracy as the direct opposite of Metallica's: indifference. "It's tricky," Ira says, "because, you know, you wanna make a living doing this and it'd be nice if people actually bought the music. But on the other hand, there's kinda nothing you can do about it."[7] The band has adopted a similar attitude toward other changes in the music industry they have no power over; for example, when asked if he was worried about the effect Spotify was having on the band's income, Ira responded by saying, "We're just pretty successful at not thinking about it."[8] It's part of the reason why Yo La Tengo decided to go managerless in the mid-nineties—they weren't interested in obsessing over things they couldn't control. If anything, such an obsession was only going to damage the band even more. Instead, they focused on the things they could control, like their music.

While most major labels saw MP3s as a threat, many independent ones approached it as an opportunity to forge a deeper connection with their artists' fans. In 1999, Matador Records started offering free MP3 downloads through their then-new website as a way of promoting upcoming releases. One of the earliest songs they offered, of course, was "Saturday," added to the site a few weeks ahead of *And Then Nothing*'s release. And when Yo La Tengo launched their own website a few years later, they decided to do something similar. Through the site's "Audio" section, fans could download singles from upcoming Yo La Tengo albums and other exclusive material. This included songs the band had written and recorded for commercials, such as a reworked version of "Tears Are in Your Eyes" they'd produced for an Orange advertisement.[9] Other areas of the site similarly demonstrated the band's interest in connecting with fans, such as the "Questions asked" page, where the trio responded to fan mail. The conversational tone of their replies further illustrates how Ira, Georgia, and James have always come across as ordinary people first and musicians second. When one fan asked for a recommendation of a good Bloody Mary spot in Hoboken, the response was this: "I would say if you like straw hats and running the risk of someone vomiting on your shoes, it's hard to beat Bahama Mama's."[10]

Rather than viewing the rise of MP3s and the internet as threats to their success, Yo La Tengo instead saw them as a way to cut out the middleman and connect with their fans directly. It was another opportunity for them to take a step closer to true independence. The band's embrace of the nineties music industry complex was always a reluctant one, and as the 2000s kicked off—and Yo La Tengo reached a new strata of success—there was less need to play by those old rules anymore. Though the band had produced a music video for each of their nineties albums, it had always felt like an obligation. You only need to watch a couple of minutes of the "Sugarcube" or "Tom Courtenay" videos to see this—both of them play like parodies of the format, twisting it as much as they possibly can while still technically functioning as music videos. By the early 2000s though, MTV's importance was beginning to slip, as demonstrated by the channel's slow shift from music videos to reality TV shows like *The Osbournes*. As a result, it made no sense for Yo La Tengo to produce a video for *And Then Nothing*, and so it became their first album in a decade not to receive one. As the internet slowly became the most important way for bands to promote themselves and interact with fans, providing advice on Bloody Mary spots was probably a much better use of Yo La Tengo's time and money than producing an expensive video that MTV might choose not to air.

If the nineties music industry had provided Yo La Tengo with a necessary launchpad for their career, by the early 2000s they had successfully used that momentum to move out of its orbit. Since the beginning, the band sought independence; all they wanted was the freedom to make music and express themselves in a way that felt true. And now, at this key point of change in the industry, it made sense for them to take that next step toward freedom. This is why, as a lead single, "Saturday" felt so representative of where Yo La Tengo were in their career. They didn't need to release a song that would appeal to radio stations or MTV, because they weren't reliant on those promotional channels anymore; instead, they released a single that clearly conveyed what *And Then Nothing* was about, handing it to fans directly through their label's website. In the same way that Yo La Tengo's music had become more emotionally honest over time, the way they were operating as a band had never been truer to who they were as people.

***

And Then Nothing went on to become Yo La Tengo's fastest selling album yet. Not only was it the band's first release to crack the US Billboard Hot 200, reaching position 138, but it also landed them on the UK Albums Chart for the first time, peaking at 78. While these stats might not seem that impressive in the grand scheme of things, they marked another milestone in Yo La Tengo's modest but ever positive growth. Nine albums deep into their career, their visibility had steadily risen with each one. There are very few, if any, acts that have managed a similar trajectory over the first seventeen years of their career. But then, Yo La Tengo's goal was never to become the biggest band in the world; their goal was to create a career that was sustainable.

Although *And Then Nothing* was reviewed positively by most critics, the initial response definitely felt cooler than that of *I Can Hear the Heart Beating as One*. Two of Yo La Tengo's biggest champions up to that point, *Village Voice* critic Robert Christgau and *Pitchfork* founder Ryan Schreiber, both seemed more reserved this time around. Describing the album as a "background tour de force,"[11] Christgau awarded it a B rating—contrasting with the As he gave their previous two releases—while Schreiber concluded, "As a whole, [...] it may be one of their less ear-catching records."[12] Still, other critics were more complementary of the album's approach, like Rob Sheffield of *Rolling Stone*. "There's no point pretending that this album will make Yo La Tengo rich and famous," he wrote. "But if the connection between rock & roll and romance still means anything to you, if guitars play a key role in your bodily chemistry, if you don't gag at the idea of record-collector geeks having sex, [...] *And Then Nothing Turned Itself Inside-Out* will open you up to intense new pleasures."[13]

By the end of the decade, even the critics who'd initially felt lukewarm on *And Then Nothing* came around. Ten years after their reserved review of the album, *Pitchfork* would rank it at thirty-seven on their list of the top 200 albums of the 2000s.[14] This feels very representative of the type of album *And Then Nothing* is: a slow burn. Though Yo La Tengo's ordinariness as people had always been a part of their music, never before had they released a set of songs that cut so close to their real lives; this involved stripping away some of the immediacy, and guitar thrashing, that had drawn in some fans in the first place. With the increased emphasis on intimate lyrics and slower, spaced-out instrumentation, it was as though they were asking audiences to listen in a way they might not have in the past. Ira, Georgia, and James were checking whether their fans were really paying attention, and the tour Yo La Tengo undertook in support of *And Then Nothing* only seemed to stress this further.

At this point, Yo La Tengo had built up a reputation as a riotous live act. Their shows were known for being loud and spontaneous; they were the sort of band that might cover a song from *The Producers* on the fly or stretch out a single jam for the entirety of their set. For the *And Then Nothing* tour, though, they decided to take a different approach. "The shows we're going to do will be much quieter than before," Ira said in an interview ahead of the tour. "We know that the songs are demanding and that the energy of a crowded rock club is not the energy of this record."[15] As a result, most of the shows on the tour took place in seated venues. The group also added two additional members to their touring band to help recreate *And Then Nothing*'s intricately layered soundscapes: David Kilgour of the Clean and Mac

McCaughan of Superchunk. These two changes almost seemed like violations of some unwritten Yo La Tengo code. In the same way the band had resisted various genre labels throughout their career, performing in seated venues and expanding beyond their core lineup showed them shrugging off their own reputation as a live act. The Yo La Tengo that fans had gone to see on previous tours was only one version of who Ira, Georgia, and James were.

For most of the dates on the tour, the band kicked things off with "Night Falls on Hoboken," their new album's lengthiest and arguably most demanding song. It also acted as the perfect mood setter for what the show would be. Though they did bring out some louder favorites throughout the tour, often during the encore, the setlists skewed heavily toward the quieter moments on *And Then Nothing* and previous releases. Songs like "From Black to Blue" and "Tears Are in Your Eyes" asked fans to listen intently, and going through recordings of shows from this tour, most audiences responded in the way Yo La Tengo wanted them to. People remained hushed during the quiet songs and paid attention to what the group had to say.

Although Ira, Georgia, and James had penned emotional songs before, the tracks on *And Then Nothing* seemed to push this side of the band to a new extreme. And their decision to fully embrace the album's emotional nakedness during these live shows says a lot about how confident the group had become. They weren't just exposing themselves to their audience on record, they were asking people to sit and watch them as they recreated those intimate moments live, over and over again.

During a Q&A session a couple of years after *And Then Nothing*'s release, one fan asked about the difficulty of performing the album's more emotionally transparent songs live, citing "The Crying of Lot G" as a specific example. "As an outsider, it would appear that it's one thing to write such a personal song and sing it one or two times into a microphone in a studio where you're surrounded by people that are close to you in your life," the fan wrote, "but then to perform that same kind of song in front of any audience would require something else."[16]

Ira's response was uncharacteristically candid. "It was definitely hard to sing while recording it, and hard to sing the first few times we played it live," he said. "But I (and I think all of us) really like the challenge […] of performing shows in which we combine overtly personal material with, say, an impromptu version of 'Hey Jude' (which is of course personal in a whole other way)."[17] Though the tour behind *And Then Nothing* highlighted the potency of the album's songs, as Ira's quote suggests, they make more sense in the context of a Yo La Tengo show with a greater array of moods. Ira the 42-year-old who wrote "The Crying of Lot G" and Ira the eleven-year-old who saw The Beatles perform "Hey Jude" on TV are both the same person; having the two songs side by side in a set only highlights how complicated and varied we all are as people. One day we're the pining teenager on "Cherry Chapstick" and the next we're the hopeless romantic on "Our Way to Fall." By expanding themselves through *And Then Nothing*, Yo La Tengo demonstrated that we never really stop discovering who we are and what we're capable of expressing.

Night Falls on Hoboken

How should bands define success? How should any type of artist define success? During their first decade, Yo La Tengo was still discovering what that word meant for them, which might explain why it took them so long to gain momentum. Perhaps in those early days, when Ira and Georgia were playing Velvet Underground covers for their friends at Maxwell's, success simply meant being able to perform in front of a crowd without their hands shaking or voices quivering. Later, when the duo were writing songs for *Ride the Tiger*, maybe it meant actually releasing an album and being able to tour behind it. And when the band received those initial waves of critical attention with *Fakebook*, perhaps success was one day being able to leave behind their freelance writing and editing gigs and making Yo La Tengo their full-time jobs.

The string of four albums the group released between 1993 and 2000—*Painful, Electr-O-Pura, I Can Hear the Heart Beating as One*, and *And Then Nothing Turned Itself Inside-Out*—are often viewed as the high point of their career, and I think this has to do with them landing on a final meaning of what success meant for them. Yo La Tengo did not only find their voice with these albums, they realized they needed to prioritize that voice above everything else. If they simply focused on making music that was true to who they were, then every other definition of success would eventually come along with it. "The success of this band, or however you want to describe that," Georgia says, "is that I think we do follow what we want to do and follow instinctively what we want to play musically. And when people respond, it's great, but we still basically do what we want and what we respond to."[1]

Yo La Tengo's music from this period onward can be viewed as an extension of the band members' lives. While there's an emotional distance between Ira and Georgia as people and Ira and Georgia as musicians on "The River of Water," by the time they were writing songs like "Our Way to Fall" and "The Crying of Lot G," that barrier had become paper thin. This is why *And Then Nothing* felt not only like a culmination of the three albums that preceded it, but also the band's entire discography up to that point. And there's something inspiring about the way this peak in vulnerability lined up with the band's peak in acclaim. *And Then Nothing* wouldn't go on to be quite as commercially and critically successful as *I Can Hear*, yet the one-two punch of these albums is what helped secure Yo La Tengo's legacy. Only a few years after *And Then Nothing*'s release, they were being described as a band with "nothing left to prove"[2] and an "indie institution."[3] In 2002, they were even immortalized in an article from the satirical news site *The Onion*: "37 Record-Store Clerks Feared Dead in Yo La Tengo Concert Disaster."[4]

By the time *And Then Nothing* came out, Yo La Tengo had already had an enviably long career. Ira and Georgia were in their forties when they started touring behind the album—for comparison, The Beatles were all in their late twenties and early thirties when the group broke up. It's one of the most remarkable and admirable things about the band: they just keep going. Though *And Then Nothing* has the mood of a late-career album, thanks to its slow pace and mature themes, at the time of the book's writing, it actually sits at the dead center of Yo La Tengo's discography. Album nine out of seventeen. And with those subsequent eight albums, Ira, Georgia, and James have only continued to develop their sound, digging even deeper into themselves and each other.

Released in 2003, the group's next album, *Summer Sun*, continued to challenge people's perception of what a Yo La Tengo record should be. Opener "Beach Party Tonight" sounded unlike anything they'd put out before. The song washes over the listener like a morning wave. There are no drums or guitars present; instead, an array of softly blown trumpets and saxophones accompany Ira's hushed vocals. It sets the tone for *Summer Sun* perfectly: an album which saw the trio invite an assortment of jazz musicians to record with them. From Roy Campbell Jr.'s trumpet to William Parker's upright bass, these fresh sonic textures helped push Yo La Tengo's sound in a completely new direction (again). The piano, an instrument the group had never really placed much focus on before, suddenly plays a central role on many of the songs, from the rollicking "Georgia Vs. Yo La Tengo" to the softly dissonant "Nothing but You and Me."

Much like their previous albums, *Summer Sun* was heavily influenced by what was happening in Ira, Georgia, and James's lives at the time. Georgia's mother had passed away just as the group started work on the record, and her old piano ended up marooned in their practice space, which is why the instrument feels like the sun all the songs are orbiting. These circumstances also had a huge influence on the mood of *Summer Sun*, which, despite its balmy title, might be even more downbeat than *And Then Nothing*. There's a sense of longing to many of the songs; "Today is the Day" sees Georgia daydreaming about someone she can no longer reach, and on "Season of the Shark" Ira sings about lending strength to a struggling friend. "Do you need someone to hide behind?" he sings. "Well, I don't mind, well, I don't mind." Unlike *And Then Nothing*, though, these heavier themes don't jump out immediately. Just as that album's sparse instrumentation seemed to underline its lyrics, the busier mood of *Summer Sun* obscured them somewhat. Still, the deeper you dig into it, the more you realize it's just as emotionally naked as *And Then Nothing*. "I'd say this record is about coping," Ira says. "I don't think it's a particularly despairing record, but I'm not sure how upbeat it is."[5]

Despite the album highlighting a new side of the band, both lyrically and musically, it was received much less warmly than their previous few releases; some critics even deemed it their weakest outing since the eighties.[6] In particular, *Pitchfork*, the publication that had helped lift Yo La Tengo in the first place, seemed to turn on them fully. "Can there exist a fate worse than mediocrity for a band that's had a taste of greatness?" Eric Carr's review opened. "[It] consistently reaches a height of disposability so static and homogenous that it simply must be dispersed over an hour's worth of music. This isn't the sound of one of the most prominent institutions in independent music maturing; it's more like decomposing."[7] This negative reception feels less like a reflection of *Summer Sun*'s actual quality and more how high the band had been riding up to that point. For the past ten years of their career, they'd been a critical darling—they were almost due for a backlash. And that backlash, ultimately, felt like part of the journey the band had been on since they first chose to go managerless almost a decade ago: it was another step toward independence. By breaking away from the critics that had first championed them, they proved they were free from everyone's expectations except their own.

***

When it comes to the albums Yo La Tengo has released since *And Then Nothing*, "Night Falls On Hoboken" has always seemed like a fitting metaphor to me. Across that song's seventeen minutes, the trio keeps things interesting with small instrumental shifts; Ira starts looping his guitar's feedback, James swaps his bass out for an organ, a second drum kit is introduced... Throughout all of this, though, the core of the song remains the same, just as the core of Yo La Tengo's music has always remained the same, even as they indulge in slight switch-ups on every subsequent release. Although *Summer Sun* is colored by brass flourishes and romping piano chords—sounds people wouldn't have associated with the band previously—the album is still built around Ira, Georgia, and James. Their bond remains the indestructible center of every Yo La Tengo release.

After *Summer Sun*, the band moved in a noisier direction with the wonderfully titled *I Am Not Afraid of You and*

I Will Beat Your Ass. On top of featuring some of Yo La Tengo's heaviest songs in over a decade, it also saw the band exploring even more new sonic textures, such as trombones, euphoniums, and a newly discovered falsetto from Ira. Then, on the album after that, *Popular Songs*, the group indulged in a more orchestral sound, with cinematic string sections showing up on several songs. It has the atmosphere of a lush, expansive sixties pop album. Each release since has involved similar pivots—from the borderline ambient musings of *There's a Riot Going On* to the improvised drones of *We Have Amnesia Sometimes*—while still remaining recognizably Yo La Tengo. In small ways, these albums continue to expand the audience's understanding of who this band is.

This is something the trio have continued to do as live performers as well, acting as a backing band for a number of different musicians—Yoko Ono, Ray Davies, Aesop Rock—while continuing to experiment with their own show. My favorite example of this is the Wheel of Fate tour they undertook in 2010. The format was simple: instead of a support act, the first half of each show would be determined by the spin of a giant wheel, à la *Wheel of Fortune*. The audience might be treated to an array of Yo La Tengo songs specifically beginning with the letter S, a performance of the band's soundtrack for the Jean Painley documentary *The Sounds of Science*, or even a set from James's solo side-project Dump. Perhaps the most infamous option though was "Sitcom Theatre." When the wheel landed on it, Ira, Georgia, and James would gather on stage to act out an episode of a sitcom, reading out the whole script. What seemed like an entertaining idea on paper proved more testing for the audience when, during the Chicago stop of the tour, the wheel landed on it. The trio proceeded to act out "The Chinese Restaurant" episode of *Seinfeld*, each of them playing a different character. "There was one person right at the beginning, right up front," Ira remembers. "She just goes, 'This is my worst fucking nightmare.'"[8] Still, despite this reaction, the band committed to the bit. They read through the entire script.

Although Yo La Tengo's music has inspired a number of artists over the years—they've been covered by everyone from Bon Iver to the Flaming Lips—it's arguably their approach to being a band that's been the biggest source of influence. Over the past couple of decades, and especially since 2020, it's become increasingly difficult for musicians to make a living from their music. Even members of established mid-sized bands often have to supplement their income with side-gigs. And though Yo La Tengo's success has bobbed up and down in the years since *And Then Nothing*—some albums sold less well than others, some tour concepts were less well-received than others—they always seem to be propelled forward by the belief that things will work out in the end. And their career seems to prove that it does. Even if *Summer Sun* broke the steady commercial trajectory the band had maintained since the beginning of their career, their thirteenth album, 2013's *Fade*, went on to become their highest charting album yet, landing at fourteen on the Billboard Albums chart. This was thirty years deep into their career. It's the way Yo La Tengo have continued to thrive, all while never compromising who they are, that makes them the ideal American band for so many other musicians.

I think this honesty is something any type of artist can take away from the band. It's an old adage that you should make art for yourself first and others second, but the way Yo La Tengo have constructed a creative life for themselves seems to exemplify that. It is through that integrity they've amassed a certain level of respect from their fans. "When we started, I truly don't think we ever thought that anyone would listen," Ira says. "Sometimes, even to this day, I feel kind of equally mystified that anyone's listening. We're just fortunate enough that enough of the people who like our band appreciate the fact that we like trying different things and are willing to fall on our face."[9]

When I was younger, I used to think The Beatles had the ideal creative career. It was succinct, tight, and romantic; one where a lot of things happened in a short space of time and everything felt incomprehensibly big. In a similar way, there's a certain perverse attraction to how the lives and careers of artists like Kurt Cobain and Jimi Hendrix ended so suddenly, before they had the chance to release a poorly received album. I don't feel the same way about these types of careers anymore. No one wants the height of their acclaim compressed into a few years, or to have to die to solidify their legendary status. There's something beautiful about a short and sharp career, yes, but a good story is not the same thing as a good creative life. And it's the latter that the members of Yo La Tengo have achieved.

***

When I last saw Yo La Tengo live, they only played a single song from *And Then Nothing*. Ironically, it was the song that felt like it belonged on the album the least: "Cherry Chapstick." Still, the band's set spanned the entirety of their history. Songs dating as far back as the mid-eighties sat comfortably alongside ones from more recent albums; the feedback-laden ending of "Serpentine"—a *New Wave Hot Dogs* deep-cut—bled seamlessly into "Brain Capers," a distorted rocker from their latest album, *This Stupid World.* There was something remarkable about the way the band honored all their eras, sometimes prioritizing tracks even the most diehard Yo La Tengo fans weren't familiar with over their most well-known numbers. Though they didn't play it at the specific show I was at, even "The River of Water," the band's very first single, made an appearance on the tour.

Despite having less-than-positive feelings about some of their early material, Yo La Tengo accept all of their discography as part of who they are. Life is like that: it's full of ups and downs, highs and lows, and all of them, it can be argued, equally define who we are. Each piece of music Yo La Tengo have released documents not only their journey as a band, but their lives as well, and they understand that all of it matters. Even as a band that always looks forward— operating on the belief that each album they release is their best one yet—they appreciate that it's everything that happened before that brought them to that point.

The most moving moment of the show came about halfway through, when the band played a song that was over thirty years old. Georgia put down her drumsticks and joined Ira at the front of the stage, as he gently started strumming some chords on an acoustic guitar. Then James came in with a plodding bassline. It was only when Ira and Georgia started crooning the song's opening lines that the audience realized what they were playing. "Let's be undecided," they sang, "let's take our time."

In 1993, "Big Day Coming" felt like the band's mission statement, and three decades later it still does. The version the band played was utterly distinct from the two that appeared on *Painful*; stripped back and delicately delivered, the power of the song's lyrics only seemed to be heightened. "There's a big day coming," Ira and Georgia sang together, "and I can hardly wait." Of course, those words seem to take on a different meaning now; when Ira and Georgia initially wrote them, they hadn't found a permanent bassist yet and they hadn't signed to Matador Records. If you asked them then, they probably wouldn't have guessed that Yo La Tengo would still be touring, let alone selling out shows, thirty years later. It lends the song a wistfulness it never had before.

Still, despite the subsequent trajectory of Yo La Tengo's career loading "Big Day Coming" with additional meaning, watching the band perform it, I think the song's original sentiment still applies. Even forty years deep into their career, you can sense that Ira, Georgia, and James still operate on the belief that there are thousands of big days yet to come.

Acknowledgments

A lot of people are responsible for this book existing, some directly and some indirectly. I want to thank my family for always encouraging me to write and showing interest in my work, even when it required them to listen to a semi-obscure, hour-long indie rock album: all my friends in Bristol and Leipzig, for listening to me talk about Yo La Tengo for months on end while working on this book; Justine, for reading the initial proposal and encouraging me to send it; and Olly, for providing critical feedback on the first proper draft.

I'd also like to thank all the editors who have published my music reviews over the years, including Jon Kean, Mustafa Mirreh, Melanie Smith, Naomi Dryden-Smith, and Rachel Morris. In many ways, this book feels like the culmination of all that writing. Additionally, I'm grateful to everyone at Bloomsbury, including Leah Babb-Rosenfeld and my editor Ryan Pinkard for believing in this book and wanting to put it out into the world.

Finally, thank you to Yo La Tengo. Without your music, there wouldn't have been a book to write.

Notes

Introduction

1. "100 Best Albums of the '90s ," *Rolling Stone*, October 4, 2019, https://www.rollingstone.com/music/music-lists/100-best-albums-of-the-90s-152425/.

2. Robert Christgau, "Beating as One: Yo La Tengo Make Their Love Album," *Robert Christgau Consumer Guide*, April 15, 2003, http://www.robertchristgau.com/xg/rock/yolateng-03.php.

3. Michael James Hall, "This Stupid World," *Under the Radar*, February 14, 2023, https://www.undertheradarmag.com/reviews/this_stupid_world_yo_la_tengo/.

4. Jem Aswad, "Nearly Four Decades in, Yo La Tengo Reaches a New Peak with 'This Stupid World': Album Review," *Variety,* February 14, 2023, https://variety.com/2023/music/album-reviews/yo-la-tengo-this-stupid-world-album-review-1235519418/.

5. "Yo La Tengo Tour Statistics: This Stupid World," *setlist.fm*, accessed March 1, 2024, https://www.setlist.fm/stats/yo-la-tengo-7bd6ae90.html.

6. Gerard Cosloy, "Episode 07—Yo La Tengo on 'I Can Hear the Heart Beating as One,'" *The Matador Revisionist Podcast*, podcast episode, July 12, 2022, https://podcasts.apple.com/us/podcast/yo-la-tengo-on-i-can-hear-the-heart-beating-as-one.

7. Ibid.

8. Jason Josephes, "Yo La Tengo: I Can Hear the Heart Beating as One," *Pitchfork*, April 22, 1997, http://www.pitchforkmedia.com/record-reviews/y/yo-la-tengo/i-can-hear-the-heart.shtml, archived November 5, 2005, at the Wayback Machine.

Everyday

1. Sun Ra and His Intergalactic Arkestra, "At First There Was Nothing," track 3 on *Outer Space Employment Agency*, compact disc, Total Energy, 1999.

2. Alyssa Loh and Alma Vescovi, "Interview with Photographer Gregory Crewdson," *The American Reader*, accessed March 1, 2024, https://theamericanreader.com/interview-with-photographer-gregory-crewdson/.

3. Jessie Jarnow, *Big Day Coming: Yo La Tengo and the Rise of Indie Rock* (New York: Gotham Press, 2012).

4. Ohio University School of Media Arts & Studies, "An Afternoon with Ira Kaplan of Yo La Tengo," YouTube video, October 3, 2013, https://www.youtube.com/watch?v=5U10ATkdSWU&t=555s.

5. Jamie Lang, "On Take Your Child to Work Day, Emily Hubley Talks Three Generations of Family Animation," *Cartoon Brew*, April 28, 2022, https://www.cartoonbrew.com/classic/emily-hubley-john-faith-max-rosenthal-215652.html.

6. Chris Norris, "It Takes Three to Tengo," *New York Magazine*, May 12, 1997, 50.

7. Michael Gallucci, "Two Hearts Beat as One," *Cleveland Scene*, April 6, 2000, https://www.clevescene.com/music/two-hearts-beat-as-one-1473987.

8. Rob Brunner, "And Then Nothing Turned Itself Inside-Out," *Entertainment Weekly*, February 28, 2000, https://ew.com/article/2000/02/28/and-then-nothing-turned-itself-inside-out/.

9. Steve Bodow, "Ira Kaplan," *BOMB Magazine*, April 30, 2000, https://bombmagazine.org/articles/ira-kaplan/.

10. Kerry Laureman, "The Way We Live Now: 2-6-00: Questions for Yo La Tengo; Band Mates," *The New York Times*, February 6, 2000, https://www.nytimes.com/2000/02/06/magazine/the-way-we-live-now-2-6-00-questions-for-yo-la-tengo-band-mates.html.

11. Ibid.

12. Marc Maron, "Episode 657: Ira Kaplan / Bob Odenkirk & David Cross," *WTF with Marc Maron*, podcast audio, November 23, 2015, https://www.wtfpod.com/podcast/episodes/episode_657_-_ira_kaplan_bob_odenkirk_david_cross.

13. Mark Athitakis, "Yo La Tengo with Quickspace," *Riverfront Times*, March 29, 2000, https://www.riverfronttimes.com/music/yo-la-tengo-with-quickspace-2474760.

14. Tom Pinnock, "Yo La Tengo: 'Success Gave Us the Courage to Be Weirder,'" *Uncut*, August 28, 2020, https://www.uncut.co.uk/features/yo-la-tengo-success-gave-us-the-courage-to-be-weirder-127796/.

Our Way to Fall

1. Chris Nelson, "Yo La Tengo Turn Themselves Inside-Out," *MTV News*, February 18, 2000, https://www.mtv.com/news/sjdyi1/yo-la-tengo-turn-themselves-inside-out.

2. Mark Athitakis, "Yo La Tengo with Quickspace," *Riverfront Times*, March 29, 2000, https://www.riverfronttimes.com/music/yo-la-tengo-with-quickspace-2474760.

3. Joshua Minsoo Kim, "James McNew (Yo La Tengo)," *Tone Glow*, October 8, 2020, https://toneglow.substack.com/p/0345-james-mcnew-yo-la-tengo.

4. Ibid.

5. shaxan, "Yo La Tengo's Ira Kaplan and Georgia Hubley @ Overheard w/ Evan Smith," YouTube video, February 20, 2019, https://www.youtube.com/watch?v=Ko7VU4qry8U.

6. Steve Klinge, "The Making of Yo La Tengo's 'Painful,'" *Magnet Magazine*, March 3, 2017, https://magnetmagazine.com/2017/03/03/magnet-classics-the-making-of-yo-la-tengos-painful/.

7. Ohio University School of Media Arts & Studies, "An Afternoon with Ira Kaplan of Yo La Tengo," YouTube video, October 3, 2013, https://www.youtube.com/watch?v=5U10ATkdSWU&t=555s.

8. Stuart Berman, "Extra Painful," *Pitchfork*, December 2, 2014, https://pitchfork.com/reviews/albums/20017-yo-la-tengo-extra-painful/.

9. Michael Nelson, "Yo La Tengo Albums From Worst to Best," *Stereogum*, October 12, 2012, https://www.stereogum.com/1169501/yo-la-tengo-albums-from-worst-to-best/.

10. Ohio University School of Media Arts & Studies, "An Afternoon with Ira Kaplan of Yo La Tengo."

11. Kim, "James McNew (Yo La Tengo)."

Let's Save Tony Orlando's House

1. Lou Stathis, "Out to Lynch," *Heavy Metal*, October, 1982, 8.

2. David Browne, "Hoboken's Finest," *New York Magazine*, September 10, 2009, https://nymag.com/arts/popmusic/features/58966/.

3. Tom Pinnock, "Yo La Tengo: 'Success Gave Us the Courage to Be Weirder,'" *Uncut*, August 28, 2020, https://www.uncut.co.uk/features/yo-la-tengo-success-gave-us-the-courage-to-be-weirder-127796/.

4. Benjamin Cook, "Ira Kaplan Reflects on Four Decades of Yo La Tengo," *Huck*, October 22, 2020, https://www.huckmag.com/article/ira-kaplan-reflects-on-four-decades-of-yo-la-tengo.

5. Robert Christgau, "Yo La Tengo," *Robert Christgau Consumer Guide*, accessed March 1, 2024, https://www.robertchristgau.com/get_artist.php?name=yo+la+tengo.

6. Ian King, "Electr-o-pura (25th Anniversary Reissue)," *Under the Radar*, September 17, 2020, https://www.undertheradarmag.com/reviews/yo_la_tengo_electr-o-pura_25th_anniversary_reissue.

7. Ben Beaumont-Thomas, "Yo La Tengo on Their Greatest Hits: 'Maybe No One Else Is Listening,'" *The Guardian*, March 16, 2018, https://www.theguardian.com/music/2018/mar/16/yo-la-tengo-on-their-greatest-hits-maybe-no-one-else-is-listening.

8. Iker Seisdedos, "Yo La Tengo: Four Decades as Indie Rock as Couple's Therapy," *EL PAÍS*, April 30, 2023, https://english.elpais.com/culture/2023-04-30/yo-la-tengo-four-decades-of-indie-rock-as-couples-therapy.html.

9. Craig Marks and Rob Tannenbaum, "The Hoboken Sound: An Oral History of Maxwell's," *Vulture*, July 21, 2013, https://www.vulture.com/2013/07/hoboken-sound-an-oral-history-of-maxwells.html.

Last Days of Disco

1. Allison Stuart, "Alternative Nation's Last Stand: Lollapalooza 1995, an Oral History," *Washington Post*, August 11, 2015, https://www.washingtonpost.com/lifestyle/style/alternative-nations-last-stand-lollapalooza-1995-an-oral-history/2015/08/10/cb6857e4-3087-11e5-8f36-18d1d501920d_story.html.

2. Ibid.

3. Ohio University School of Media Arts & Studies, "An Afternoon with Ira Kaplan of Yo La Tengo," YouTube video, October 3, 2013, https://www.youtube.com/watch?v=5U10ATkdSWU&t=555s.

4. Stephen Thompson, "Yo La Tengo," *AV Club*, March 22, 2000, https://www.avclub.com/yo-la-tengo-1798208045.

5. Gerard Cosloy, "Episode 07—Yo La Tengo on 'I Can Hear the Heart Beating as One,'" *The Matador Revisionist Podcast*, podcast episode, July 12, 2022, https://podcasts.apple.com/us/podcast/yo-la-tengo-on-i-can-hear-the-heart-beating-as-one.

6. Chris Nelson, "Yo La Tengo Turn Themselves Inside-Out," *MTV News*, February 8, 2000, https://www.mtv.com/news/sjdyi1/yo-la-tengo-turn-themselves-inside-out.

7. Micajah Henley, "Issue #97: Yo La Tengo," *Bandbox*, July 19, 2023, 13.

8. Lij Shaw, "Episode 70: Roger Moutenot—Producing Yo La Tengo & Paula Cole," *Recording Studio Rockstars*, podcast episode, January 6, 2017, https://recordingstudiorockstars.com/rsr070-roger-moutenot-producing-yo-la-tengo-paula-cole/.

Nothing Turned Itself Inside-Out …

1. Eric Weisbard, "This Monkey's Gone to Heaven," *Spin*, July 1998, 64.

2. *Spin*, July 1998, 1.

3. Gerard Cosloy, "Episode 07—Yo La Tengo on 'I Can Hear the Heart Beating As One,'" *The Matador Revisionist Podcast*, podcast episode, July 12, 2022, https://podcasts.apple.com/us/ podcast/yo-la-tengo-on-i-can-hear-the-heart-beating-as-one.

4. Ibid.

5. Tom Pinnock, "Yo La Tengo: 'Success Gave Us the Courage to Be Weirder,'" *Uncut*, August 28, 2020, https://www.uncut.co.uk/features/yo-la-tengo-success-gave-us-the-courage-tobe-weirder-127796/.

6. Steve Klinge, "The Making of Yo La Tengo's 'Painful,'" *Magnet Magazine*, March 3, 2017, https://magnetmagazine.com/2017/03/03/magnet-classics-the-making-of-yo-latengos-painful/.

7. Jesse Jarnow, "Yo La Tengo: Our Life in 15 Songs," *Rolling Stone*, August 27, 2015, https://www.rollingstone.com/music/music-lists/yo-la-tengo-our-life-in-15-songs-63829/.

8. Kevin Robinson, "Roger Moutenot: New York to Nashville," *Tape Op: The Book about Creative Music Recording, Vol. II*, ed. Larry Crane (Winona: Hal Leonard Corporate, 2007), 123. 8.

9. Ben Beaumont-Thomas, "Yo La Tengo on Their Greatest Hits: 'Maybe No One Else Is Listening,'" *The Guardian*, 2018.

10. Ohio University School of Media Arts & Studies, "An Afternoon with Ira Kaplan of Yo La Tengo," YouTube video, October 3, 2013, https://www.youtube.com/watch?v=5U10AT kdSWU&t=555s.

… And Became Something

1. "U.S. Music Revenue Database," *RIAA*, accessed March 1, 2024, https://www.riaa.com/u-s-sales-database/.

2. Ibid.

3. Stephen Witt, "The Man Who Broke the Music Business," *The New Yorker*, April 20, 2015, https://www.newyorker.com/magazine/2015/04/27/the-man-who-broke-the-music-business.

4. Ibid.

5. "U.S. Music Revenue Database."

6. Tyler Golsen, "Metallica vs Napster: The Moment Music on the Internet Changed Forever," September 3, 2023, https://faroutmagazine.co.uk/metallica-vs-napster-music-internet-changed/.

7. shaxan, "Yo La Tengo's Ira Kaplan and Georgia Hubley @ Overheard w/ Evan Smith," YouTube video, February 20, 2019, https://www.youtube.com/watch?v=Ko7VU4qry8U.

8. Ibid.

9. "YO LA TENGO SELLOUT: Part Three," *Yo La Tengo*, accessed March 1, 2024, http://www.yolatengo.com/sellout/index.html, archived April 3, 2005, at the Wayback Machine.

10. "January 2003: We Answer Your Questions," Yo La Tengo, accessed March 1, 2024, http://www.yolatengo.com/lettersJan03.html, archived April 3, 2005, at the Wayback Machine.

11. Robert Christgau, "Yo La Tengo," *Robert Christgau Consumer Guide*, accessed March 1, 2024, https://www.robertchristgau.com/get_artist.php?name=yo+la+tengo.

12. Ryan Schreiber, "And Then Nothing Turned Itself Inside-Out," *Pitchfork*, February 29, 2000, https://pitchfork.com/reviews/albums/8870-and-then-nothing-turned-itself-inside-out/.

13. Rob Sheffield, "And Then Nothing Turned Itself Inside-Out," *Rolling Stone*, March 2, 2000, https://www.rollingstone.com/music/music-album-reviews/and-then-nothing-turned-itself-inside-out-191430/.

14. "The Best 200 Albums of the 2000s," *Pitchfork*, October 2, 2009, https://pitchfork.com/features/lists-and-guides/7710-the-top-200-albums-of-the-2000s-20-1/.

15. Steve Bodow, "Ira Kaplan," *BOMB Magazine*, April 30, 2000, https://bombmagazine.org/articles/ira-kaplan/.

16. "Yo La Tengo," *Washington Post*, April 8, 2003, https://web.archive.org/web/20070213050240/http:/discuss.

washingtonpost.com/wp-srv/zforum/03/sp_entertainment_
kaplan040803.htm, archived February 13, 2007, at the
Wayback Machine.

17. Ibid.

Night Falls on Hoboken

1. shaxan, "Yo La Tengo's Ira Kaplan and Georgia Hubley @
Overheard w/ Evan Smith," YouTube video, February 20, 2019,
https://www.youtube.com/watch?v=Ko7VU4qry8U.

2. Jenni Cole, "Yo La Tengo—I Am Not Afraid of You and I Will
Beat Your Ass," *Music OMH*, September 11, 2006, https://
www.musicomh.com/reviews/albums/yo-la-tengo-i-am-not-
afraid-of-you-and-i-will-beat-your-ass.

3. Vladimir Wormwood, "I Am Not Afraid of You and I Will
Beat Your Ass," *Drowned in Sound*, September 21, 2006,
https://drownedinsound.com/releases/8106/reviews/1156942-
yo-la-tengo-i-am-not-afraid-of-you-and-i-will-beat-your-ass.

4. "37 Record-Store Clerks Feared Dead in Yo La Tengo Concert
Disaster," *The Onion*, April 10, 2002, https://www.theonion.
com/37-record-store-clerks-feared-dead-in-yo-la-tengo-
conce-1819566399.

5. Jim DeRogatis, "Yo La Tengo Still Growing with 'Summer
Sun,'" *Jimdero*, June 6, 2003, https://www.jimdero.com/
News2003/June6YoLaTengo.htm.

6. Elizabeth Nelson, "Yo La Tengo Albums from Worst to
Best," *Stereogum*, April 22, 2022, https://www.stereogum.
com/2177931/yo-la-tengo-albums-ranked-worst-to-best/lists/
counting-down/.

---

7. Eric Carr, "Summer Sun," *Pitchfork*, April 9, 2003, https://pitchfork.com/reviews/albums/8864-summer-sun/.

8. Triple R 102.7FM, "Ira Kaplan (Yo La Tengo)—Interview at Golden Plains 2014 (Live at 3RRR)," YouTube video, March 18, 2014, https://www.youtube.com/watch?v=ibVDqnV4yRQ.

9. Liberty Dunworth, "Yo La Tengo's Ira Kaplan on the Changing Music Scene and Refusing to Rely on Others to Convey Your Vision," *Guitar.com*, February 1, 2023, https://guitar.com/features/interviews/yo-la-tengo-ira-kaplan-new-album-this-stupid-world/.